ENTREPRENEURSHIP FOR LEADERS

INDIGORIVER
PUBLISHING

the For Leaders

SERIES

BOOK 1

Entrepreneurship for Leaders

10 SUCCESS KEYS TO ELEVATE YOU TO THE NEXT LEVEL

Joel Clelland, Bobby Dunaway, Matthew Holland,

Jason Duncan, Mark Hayes, Michael Markiewicz,

Ellen Moran, Daniel Vega, Jayshree Vakil, & Dan Young

EDITED BY DEBORAH FROESE

Entrepreneurship for Leaders

© 2023 by Indigo River Publishing.

The *For Leaders* series concept and design are the property of Indigo
River Publishing.

Library of Congress Control Number: 2023940616
ISBN: 978-1-954676-47-3 (print)   978-1-954676-57-2 (ebook)

Editors: Marci Carson, Deborah Froese
Cover and Interior Design: Emma Elzinga

Printed in the United States of America
First Edition

3 West Garden Street, Ste. 718
Pensacola, FL 32502
www.indigoriverpublishing.com

Ordering Information:
Quantity sales: Special discounts are available on quantity purchases by corporations,
associations, and others. For details, contact the publisher at the address above.
Orders by U.S. trade bookstores and wholesalers: Please contact the publisher at the
address above.

With Indigo River Publishing, you can always expect great books, strong voices, and
meaningful messages. Most importantly, you'll always find . . . *words worth reading.*

CONTENTS

INTRODUCTION

Welcome to the inaugural volume of the *For Leaders* series. Designed to encourage strong leadership in every walk of life, the series offers wisdom from established business and community trailblazers on a variety of leadership topics.

The idea to create *For Leaders* took root through several discussions around Indigo River Publishing's boardroom table. How could we publish a meaningful and helpful resource, something that could help experienced professionals expand and grow while allowing us to grow along with them? With our connections to a wide network of successful business and community leaders, *For Leaders* emerged as a natural choice. In this series, each volume will benefit contributors by providing them with a platform to share insights gleaned through hard work and experience from a wide array of backgrounds—education, coaching, sales, entrepreneurship, and more. It benefits readers by exposing them to the insights of successful leaders.

Most people are familiar with the *For Dummies* series (John Wily and Sons) and the *Idiot's Guide Series* (Penguin Random House). Both aim to provide entry-level information on a variety of topics. *For Leaders* is different. It targets readers who have already achieved a level of success in their endeavors and wish to enhance their leadership skills. It's a kind of book-in-hand mentorship program.

Leadership is about more than standing at the front of the crowd and yelling "charge!" As a young entrepreneurial friend told me, "It's about developing keen self-awareness and knowing your values. When you've got that figured out, you can draw from your experience and observations to empower, inspire, and encourage others."

Strong leaders are essential to success in every area of life. They illuminate purpose, build consensus, and empower their teams to achieve a unified goal. With *For Leaders,* we bring insights and tools to deepen your leadership journey.

The first volume, *Entrepreneurship for Leaders,* arrives at an auspicious time. Entrepreneurship is on the rise. After an initial lull in business applications at the beginning of the COVID-19 pandemic, new business start-ups increased dramatically. In his working paper on the status of new business startups during the pandemic, John C. Haltiwanger, a University of Maryland economist, noted that, nationwide, between the last half of 2020 and the first half of 2021, the number of startup applicants rose by more than 20% over the previous year—a rise that outpaces anything previously recorded. Summarizing this new growth, the National Bureau of Economic Research states:

Three-quarters of the recent surge in start-ups was concentrated in just 10 industries, including Non-store Retail, which accounted for a third of the growth, Personal, Professional, Food Services, and Truck Transportation. The rapid growth of likely nonemployer start-ups, which reflects self-employment activity, highlights the increasing importance of gig workers in the modern economy.

Increasingly, entrepreneurship appeals to younger people who may be dissatisfied with low pay, fewer employment opportunities, a growing disregard for "big business," or the desire to take advantage of online possibilities. "Young people [millennials] are more entrepreneurial than ever, starting twice as many businesses as the baby boomer generation according to recent data," reports the Centre for Entrepreneurs.

Consisting of ten chapters, each written by a different contributor, *Entrepreneurship for Leaders* explores a variety of topics that are sure to intersect with every leader's experience at some point along their journey. With so many different perspectives and voices, the content will vary wildly—from contrasting the differences between employees and entrepreneurs by drawing upon a classic Christmas movie to an in-depth examination of various leadership styles and how to best harness them.

We trust you'll find something that resonates in these pages.

Times are changing, and entrepreneurs are leading the way.

Deborah Froese
Executive Editor
Indigo River Publishing
June 07, 2023

CHAPTER 1

CRUSH FEAR

Jayshree Vakil

Co-Founder and CMO at Permissioned Networks, Inc.

I'll tell you what freedom is to me. No fear.
– Nina Simone

A young man moved to a new city to live with relatives. To make ends meet, he took menial jobs selling newspapers and polishing shoes on the street. Orphaned at a young age, his biggest fear was losing his livelihood. He wanted to go to college and start his own business, but he had no capital. He was afraid that striking out on his own would bring destitution and failure. He was literally impeded and crippled by his fear.

Oh, if only fear never existed, and we could all live in freedom! But fear does exist, and overcoming it builds the resilience that carries a person forward.

The Oxford dictionary defines resilience as "toughness" and the capacity to recover quickly from difficulties. But a second definition refers to "elasticity," the ability of a substance or object to spring back into shape. This latter definition is the one that characterizes resilient people and businesses, and it is the one that I want to emphasize when exploring the concept of crushing fear.

Dealing with fear requires the ability to stay true to your shape—the form of your actions and values. With over 40 years in business and entrepreneurship, I have witnessed many resilient individuals and companies, and I have also seen many who fell short in critical situations. Given my own personal demographic as an Indian-American woman, I have been especially alert to how women and minorities react to difficult situations.

Overcoming poverty and racial and sexual discrimination, the legendary Nina Simone forged a career as a jazz vocalist and became a civil rights activist. Hers was a story of resilience.

Was she ever afraid of the obstacles in front of her?

Of course, she was. Fear could have easily derailed her, but, in her own words, she overcame it by "knowing that things would change, and it was a question of keeping myself together until they did."

With her music she would go on to inspire artists ranging from John Lennon and Elton John to Aretha Franklin, Mary J. Blige, and Alicia Keys. Her social activism blazed a path that opened opportunities for other women.

History is replete with examples of men and women demonstrating resilience in the face of fear. That fear can be related to physical danger, economic deprivation, or illness. Individuals also suffer from internal fear caused by self-doubt or low self-esteem, feeling unprepared, or other similar issues, which must be overcome. Being afraid almost always results in reduced personal effectiveness whether giving up and abandoning a plan of action, stopping personal growth, or failing to engage with peers, colleagues, or other business associates. If the manifestation of these outcomes is not recognized, then fear grows until. When one is unable to separate perceived circumstances from reality, any problems or shortcomings will seem more insurmountable than they really are.

Fear is not just an individual trait. It can infect organizations and institutions too. In business, fear is due to both external and internal factors. External threats such as the competition or market conditions are easier to identify, although they may not always be easy to deal with. Identifying and addressing internal sources of fear can be more challenging because they may be ingrained in the culture. If not dealt with promptly, they can be more debilitating since they affect the overall execution of the company or institution.

Companies can develop a culture that fears failure when people leading unsuccessful initiatives are blamed in a public way or even punished via demotion or firing. This is not restricted to low-performing or mediocre companies. History is filled with examples of industry leaders who were so afraid of losing their preeminent place in their industry that they avoided taking risks or altering business models in the face of changing times.

Many years ago, I worked for Montgomery Ward, which was the indisputable leader in retail and catalog sales until the 1920s. After World War II, Sewell Avery, the leader who had rescued the company during the Depression, was so afraid of a second business downturn that he stopped all expansion and hoarded cash. That allowed Sears, Roebuck and Company to expand into growing urban suburbs and take over retail leadership.

Montgomery Ward never regained its momentum. By the time I got there it had suffered through 40 years of steady decline and eventually shut its doors in 2000.

Sometimes the fear of losing a leadership position prevents a company from making timely decisions even though market conditions and trends are moving in the opposite direction. Kodak and Polaroid lost their pre-eminent positions in photography because they stayed with physical media long after the digital revolution was evident. Xerox suffered a similar fate in copy machines.

Occasionally, a company will make a bold decision to conquer its fear and completely change its strategy. In the mid-1980s, Intel was a leader in memory chips but was facing intense price competition and losing market share to Japanese manufacturers. It could have persisted in trying to maintain its position, but instead, its leaders, Gordon Moore and Andy Grove, decided to focus on the microprocessor segment. They shut down its memory business over a couple of years. Viewed as risky at the time, that decision propelled Intel into a position that allowed them to take advantage of the PC revolution in the `80s and `90s, becoming one of the most financially lucrative companies in the world.

In defining failure and its consequences, it is important to distinguish between the implementation of a company's agreed-to strategy and tactics from new initiatives that entail risk or innovation. The former is an execution issue, failure in which could be due to either a lack of skills or effort, either of which must be addressed promptly. This is part of a normal management process and should not contribute to a fearful environment unless it is handled badly. Ideally, the latter example should be encouraged without any fear of negative consequences.

Of course, each organization's situation will be unique and require custom judgements. Repeated non-performance in new projects should also be a cause of concern.

My Story

With over 40 years of experience in business and as an entrepreneur, I am familiar with certain barriers specific to women that cause fear. When I entered the advertising business in the early 1980s, women like me were still relatively new and few. I was from India, and I had to overcome perceptions about my knowledge of the English language, American culture, and the business environment, even though I had a master's degree in advertising from Northwestern University, then— and now—one of the top advertising schools in the country. I had to confront all the glass ceiling stereotypes, many of which still exist today, albeit to a lesser degree. I had to prove that I was just as smart, just as capable of hard work, and as emotionally stable and creative as any of my male and non-minority colleagues.

But I had less freedom of movement than they did. No matter how well I performed, I was one mistake or one shortcoming away from having to prove myself all over again. In conversations with other women as well as minorities over the years, I heard the same old cliché repeatedly: you have to be twice as good to be perceived to be half as good. That attitude added to the fear and pressure I felt.

Later, when I left the corporate world and started my own advertising business, I had to work extra hard to convince clients to put their trust in me. When I chaired meetings, it was not unusual for clients to converse with my male employees rather than me.

For the last five years, as part of an organization that fosters entrepreneurship, I have had the opportunity to mentor many start-up entrepreneurs experiencing common challenges such as self-doubt (*Am I good enough?*), second-guessing themselves (*Should I be taking this risk?*), and building credibility (*Will I be taken seriously?*). While these questions may be formidable barriers to anyone, for women and minorities specifically, conquering them can seem as intimidating as climbing the mighty Andes mountain range.

I have found that entrepreneurs tend to deal with fear much better than most people because they are familiar with risk-taking. And I have learned that even when fear does arise, it can be crushed.

Five Steps to Conquer Fear

"What would you do if you weren't afraid?"

Fear is a natural reaction and nothing to be ashamed of. But it can either be debilitating or, if faced with squarely, be uplifting. Over the years, I have had to confront my own fears many times. Although I have not always been able to prevail successfully, especially early in my career, I persevered. Eventually, I developed a disciplined way to build resilience and conquer fear. It consists of five steps:

1. Recognition
2. Disinterested evaluation
3. Identifying and accentuating the positives
4. Defining a course of action
5. Continuously evaluating and adjusting

1. Recognition

Andy Grove had this to say about Intel's declining position in the memory chip business: "Many people were still holding to the 'self-evident truth' that Intel was a memory company. One of the toughest challenges is to make people see that these self-evident truths are no longer true." Recognizing fear and its source is the first step in tackling it. Sometimes this can be the hardest step of all, whether it's fear within yourself or your organization. Often the source has become embedded either in the culture or structure of an institution, as in the case of Intel. Sometimes it is because of history; it has always been done this way. Women in business and entrepreneurship have another hurdle to fear; they must deal with the traditional glass ceiling that prevents them from asking for a raise in a company or believing that their ideas won't be good enough to raise money.

How does fear manifest itself? It's different for everyone, but you can find it if you listen to your inner voice, your thoughts. Ask yourself what is really causing you to be frightened in a certain situation. You may hear, "I'm not good with people—I'm an introvert," "I don't have the skills," "What if they don't like me or think my idea is stupid?" or "What if I fail?" Procrastinating on key actions or decisions, rationalizing or excusing what you know is suboptimal behavior, or stopping your own growth or learning—these are all signs that you are afraid of something or someone.

Take the first step; admit you're afraid. Then try and identify what is behind your fear.

2. Honest Evaluation

At Intel, Andy Grove told his direct reports to "make data-based decisions and not to fear emotional opposition."

The first critical step toward crushing fear is to separate that fear from the actual reality of the situation. This requires a dispassionate evaluation. Many times, it is straightforward. If you are in a jungle and you come face-to-face with a tiger, there is no confusion. You know what is causing your fright. Similar circumstances in one's personal and business life are easy to behold, but there are many more instances when we project a fear based on possible outcomes, perceived skill shortcomings, or potential actions by external parties.

Corrie ten Boom, writer and famous Holocaust survivor, made a very perceptive observation: "Worry does not empty tomorrow of its sorrow, it empties today of its strength."

Fear has the same effect; it freezes action. It commonly magnifies perceived shortcomings or bad outcomes when facing difficult situations and leads to inaction or poor decision-making. Sometimes, the imagined negative consequences can be so debilitating that one waits until the fearful situation is resolved—positively or negatively—before moving on. By then, it's often too late to achieve a satisfactory resolution.

3. Identify and Accentuate the Positives

Once you have evaluated the source of the fear that is holding you back, and you understand its real impact, stop rationalizing past behavior. It's time to take a fresh look at your inventory of strengths and skills. What arrows in your quiver can be dispatched against the genesis of the inaction or indecision? These can be personal attributes, resources, or even other individuals.

The last asset—other individuals—is often overlooked and under-appreciated. Asking for help from others, even ones close to you, is not always easy. Ego, shame, pride, shyness, fear of rejection or ridicule are some of the emotional barriers that can prevent one from asking for aid.

For women and minorities, role models are especially important because they illuminate paths of achievement and attributes. Nina Simone's mentors were Langston Hughes, James Baldwin, and especially Lorraine Hansberry. Hansberry authored the play, *A Raisin in the Sun*. As a young African-American writer, she had earlier experienced some of the same challenges that Nina Simone faced. Because she overcame them, Simone was encouraged to do the same.

To stay with the Intel narrative, in the late 1970s, its management did a facts-based assessment of the company's strengths and weaknesses and took a cold look at market conditions. They concluded that Japanese semiconductor manufacturers were nimbler and moving faster than Intel was to develop and bring to market higher capacity memory chips at better prices. Intel had one defining asset: it was one of a handful of companies with expertise in building microprocessors, which were increasingly being used as engines in the growing personal computer market.

Although the outcome was far from certain, Intel decided to abandon the memory chip business and focus on building microprocessors. It was a gutsy and risky decision at the time, but one that management felt compelled to make. Intel succeeded beyond anyone's expectations.

4. Defining a Course of Action

Making a decision is only half the battle. Acting on it is the other, equally important, half. To do so one must define a plan of action that requires a tangible set of behaviors and relationships with concrete goals.

Construct this plan of action to exploit the strengths and skills that were identified in the previous steps. Determine how to best overcome the perceived obstacles creating fear by using your assets. Turn the challenge of overcoming problems into potential opportunities for growth. Ideally, the goals should have enough positive attributes to incentivize continuous execution of the plan.

While the need for detailed planning may be self-evident for businesses and institutions, its significance is not as obvious for individuals. Most people don't have formal structured plans for their lives. However, when faced with a major hurdle—especially one that evokes fear—it is useful to put down specific goals and a course of action to combat the challenge.

Intel had a plan of action when it decided to go all-in with the microprocessor business. In a happy co-incidence with this chapter, their initiative was called "Operation Crush." It provided a detailed blueprint on how Intel was going to enter, market, price, and otherwise compete in the market.

Nina Simone also had a plan. When she was turned down for admission to a prestigious classical music program because of her race, she was still determined to become a concert pianist. Her plan included working as an accompanist and music teacher while performing on the side in bars and on the stage. And she decided to channel her fear of discrimination into anger and activism.

5. Continuously Evaluating and Adjusting

No plan is perfect. Dwight Eisenhower acknowledged that "plans are worthless but planning is everything." There is a certain truth to this. Planning structures a course of action. It can help identify potential obstacles or skill shortages, and it helps define a clear goal or mission. However, for this discussion, I would modify Ike's quote to: "The plan is something, acting on it is everything."

There is a tendency to think that once a plan has been mapped out, the work is done—even though it has only just begun. Intel's Operation Crush worked because management emphasized execution, ensuring that all the relevant teams were trained and pointed toward a common goal: that of becoming the dominant microprocessor company in the world.

So put your plan into action and stick with it. Seeing the plan to its end and repeating it is one of the hardest habits to cultivate, but persistence is the only way the plan becomes an ingrained habit. The same challenge is found in personal behavior when individuals try to lose weight, develop new skills, save money, call mom.

Finally, be in a process of continuous improvement. That means constantly evaluating your steps and actions to see which ones are effective and which need modification or discarding and perhaps introduce new ones as required. Repetition and improvement will increase overall confidence in the plan.

Strengths and Habits: Crushing Fear at the Outset

There are a set of personal attributes and habits that, if consciously developed, will make the process above significantly easier. These concepts apply to organizations too. Among these are:

Managing time. Avoiding hard decisions almost always adds to stress. A hurried set of actions often follows procrastination, and in turn, they lead to doubt about work quality. Instead, spend adequate time on completing the most important tasks, and you will be amazed at the increase in confidence.

Managing relationships. Most people want to avoid confrontation, but sometimes fear results from a poor personal or business relationship. It could involve a superior, a peer, a spouse, or a friend. It won't always be easy, but if a relationship is the source of your discomfort, tackling it head-on is necessary. It is also unfortunately true that not all relationships are salvageable. Sometimes you have to know when to walk away.

Self-compassion. Learn not to be too hard on yourself. In many instances, your best efforts will not result in the most desired outcomes. Sometimes it may be due to a lack of appropriate skills or resources. Start to build a process of self-awareness that allows you to take an accurate inventory of your work and attributes so that you are not punishing yourself for every setback. Companies build processes to learn from their failures and can build resilience in their teams by being honest about where the shortcomings are. Individuals can too.

Other behaviors and skills will also foster positive change. The challenge is in embracing them and believing that positive change can be achieved. Imagine who you want to be in the future. You do not have to be wedded to who you are today. Take time to recognize how much you've grown and changed from your former self. These observations are reminders that growth is possible. Keep visions of who you want to become and what you want your future to be at the top of your mind. Research shows that your behavior in the present is largely shaped by your view of your future.

Make Conquering Fear a Habit

I don't want to seem too prescriptive, as if the solution to fear is formulaic and once you follow these steps, everything will work out the way that you want it to. This may not be rocket science, but it's in the doing that one achieves results, and by doing it again and again that one improves outcomes.

It has been said by many that fear can be a great motivator. I believe that the resilience built by constantly and consistently overcoming fear will turbo-charge your confidence and motivation like nothing else can do.

Remember the story of the young man I shared at the beginning of this chapter, the one whose fear of striking out on his own literally impeded and crippled him? One day he decided to take stock of his situation. He still feared the unknown and potential failure. But he also realized that his present condition wouldn't change unless he did something differently.

He later said, "I had been on the street before, and I had survived. I could do it again."

Focusing on that attitude allowed him to conquer his fear. He used the money he had managed to save and took a leap toward his dream.

He bought a single billboard—then called a "hoarding"—and used it to start an advertising business.

This is a true story. The year was 1941, and the city was Bombay (now Mumbai) in what was then Colonial British India. The company the man founded with one billboard—Green's Advertising Service Agents—grew and flourished. He ran that business successfully for 64 years, and he served as a mentor to me.

His name was Jadavkumar L. Mainthia. He was my father.

CHAPTER 2

PASSION

The Most Important Key to Success

Jason Duncan

Podcaster, Serial Entrepreneur, and Best-selling Author of Exit Without Exiting

Success usually comes to those who are too busy to be looking for it.
– Henry David Thoreau

No matter how you define success personally, there will always be someone who has a different interpretation. Some people define success by their level of fame or notoriety while others don't feel they are successful until their bank account reaches a certain number. Still, others are satisfied with a peaceful and loving home environment and the ability to spend lots of quality time with their family. It all depends on your background and what you want out of life.

Ultimately, success is directly related to achieving a desired outcome or goal. As a matter of fact, if you open any dictionary right now and look up the definition of success, you'll see references to fame, wealth, or notoriety, but the overwhelming theme of every definition indicates that success is directly related to achieving a desired outcome or goal. Plainly put, success is when you attain the results you aimed for.

Success is about results, and passion is the key to achieving them.

Passion Overcomes the Challenges of Entrepreneurship.

After interviewing literally hundreds of successful leaders and entrepreneurs from all over the world for my weekly podcast, *The Root of All Success*, I have discovered that while everyone's story is different, their journey to success is always unlocked with the same key: passion.

Passion is necessary because entrepreneurship is no walk in the park. It takes a determined mind to keep on going even when things look like they are moving in the opposite direction of your goals. People often admire the success of great entrepreneurs without recognizing the tremendous sacrifice they made to get to where they are now. If you want to be a successful entrepreneurial leader, then you should have a clear goal of what you want to accomplish, and you should strive to reach those goals with the right mindset.

If I came to you and bragged about being one of the best architects in the world but told you that I don't have a portfolio of my work, would you trust me to build your dream house? Most likely not! You want evidence to prove that I'm really up to scratch, that I can do the job. Words alone don't cut it. When it comes to success, you need to know where you're trying to go and how you're going to get there, and you have to be motivated enough to keep on sailing on your own ship.

Life takes on a whole new meaning when you see your goals and plans materialize into success. When you get to this stage, suddenly everything is possible and you're not afraid to dream big and work toward what you want in life. Success is like a breath of fresh air; you're truly living and not just coping with your day-to-day life.

You'll never find someone who has achieved a high level of success without enough passion to bring their dreams to life. Likewise, there are innumerable stories of passion-less entrepreneurs who failed.

Typically, when people talk about passion, they speak in terms of emotion. They think about someone grinding it out with a deep conviction. Excitement. Exuberance. Joy. Determination. Effort. Those are the words most closely associated with the typical definition of passion. And for good reason. Passion involves very powerful feelings ranging from love and sexual attraction to anger and hate. Passion is certainly about emotion. It's true. But there's more to it than sheer emotion.

Passion Isn't What You Think It Is.

If you look at the origin of the term *passion,* you'll find that it actually refers to suffering or enduring. It comes from a Latin word that means to endure, undergo, or experience. This is the reason we refer to Jesus's crucifixion as the "Passion of the Christ." So, passion in one sense refers to an extreme feeling or an emotion, but in another, it refers to the ability or desire to suffer or endure. Either way, it's a powerful driving force.

Do you know what you're passionate about? Building your entrepreneurial journey based on passion is one of the best things that you can do for yourself. It's not a burden to explain what you do because you're doing something that you love. You can endure, undergo, or experience whatever you need to in order to succeed, and that's what matters. You can confidently talk about what you do and build an authentic brand that is true to what you like. It's passion that gives you the motivation to keep on pushing and really helps you to set a solid foundation for your business. When you're passionate, you establish a space for yourself in which you can thrive. Then you own it.

Passion drives you toward people who have similar perspectives; it helps you to network with like-minded people who are also goal-driven and working toward a successful outcome. Think about how your passion meets your purpose in your entrepreneurial journey and work toward fulfilling it.

Are You Willing to Suffer?

Successful entrepreneurs have a powerful emotional connection to what they're doing. But they're also willing to suffer. They're willing to endure the pain and the discomfort of the launch, of the start-up, of growth—all long before they eventually reach success.

Let me tell you a story of a very successful entrepreneur who used passion to unlock tremendous success. Katie Richardson considers herself an accidental entrepreneur. She's been featured on the *Ellen DeGeneres Show*, *Rachael Ray Show*, *Today Show*, and on the cover of *Entrepreneur* magazine. Martha Stewart, Matt Damon, Camilla Alves, Mario Lopez, Robert Downey Jr., Kourtney Kardashian, Bill and Giuliana Rancic, and actress Jenna Fischer, who plays the well-known *The Office* character, Pam Beesley, are just a few of the celebrities known for using her products.

Katie created a business called Puj (pronounced pudge) almost 15 years ago. You can now find Puj in 2,000 USA stores and in 26 different countries. Her products, which are designed to make parenting babies and toddlers easier, have been sold to over one million customers around the globe. Yet, her success was not just the result of hard work—she had passion!

As a mom of two small kids under the age of three, Katie saw a need for certain products that no one else was providing so she began her business. In 2010, she took her products to a trade show. Target, Costco, Nordstrom, and other retailers were there.

Katie recounted the event during an interview with me for *The Root of All Success*. "Everyone was really curious about it [Puj] but nobody placed an order. It was devastating. I came home feeling like a total failure. I was embarrassed to talk to my family about it. I didn't even want to talk to my husband about it because it was that painful and embarrassing. I mean, we'd worked for two-plus years to develop it. And we were already paying attorneys to get it trademarked. Nobody placed an order. So, I come home from the trade show, and I felt like a complete and total failure as a designer, as a provider, and as a mother."

Being the loving and supportive husband that he was, Ben asked Katie to recount the questions that retailers at the show had asked about her products. After she shared all the questions, Ben reassured her.

"They didn't actually say no," Ben said. "They just asked you questions that we didn't have the answers to, and we just need to answer those questions and then we'll be shipping this product all over the world."

"We were standing in our cold garage, literally surrounded by all the dust and the remnants and the scraps of this harebrained idea that we've been working on for two-plus years," Katie told me. "I was wearing the same dang pair of jeans I've worn for the last five years because I couldn't even afford new outfits. I was just tired. I was cold. I was worn out. And so, when he said that . . . I was like, 'He's right!'"

Katie went back to that same trade show the following year with answers in tow. You know what? She sold out. She sold out of every sample she had and took all the orders she felt like she could handle. Puj was off to the races.

Success comes to those who have the kind of passion Katie Richardson illustrated in her story. It's about being willing to suffer through the hard times. It would've been easy for her to turn her back on the whole idea of Puj and go back to just being a mom, creating cool stuff for herself and her own kids. But her goals were about more than being a mom. She wanted to achieve great success and was willing to suffer for it. That is true passion.

Do You Have True Passion as a Leader?

Once you know what you're passionate about, dig deep and ask yourself questions that will help you to discover more about yourself and just how far you're willing to go to get where you want to be. Are you willing to suffer? Are you willing to endure the hard times? Do you have a strong emotional connection to what you're doing?

Well, here's the thing: you don't necessarily have to be passionate about your product or service in an emotional sense. My first successful entrepreneurial venture was in the LED lighting field. I wasn't passionate about LED lighting at all. As a matter of fact, I am still not passionate about LED lighting from an emotional perspective. But I've been tremendously successful in that business because I was passionate about building a business and providing a wonderful career for each of my employees. I had a strong emotional sense that building a business was something that would make an impact for my family, for my employees, and for their families. That gave me the willingness to suffer and endure. The passion that I had in building my first big company was a passionate desire to build something—not necessarily passion about the product.

Like Katie's story, my passion drove me to greater success than I could've ever imagined. Energy Lighting Services ended up being listed twice on *Inc.* magazine's list of the fastest growing privately held companies in the country. We were recognized in *Entrepreneur* magazine's list of the top 360 best entrepreneurial companies in the country. We won numerous other small business-of-the-year awards, and we were even recognized by the U.S. Federal Government as a rising star in 2014. That is because I was willing to suffer for the business. I was truly passionate!

When you aim higher, some form of sacrifice is always involved. It might be your time or giving up certain habits that are holding you back from truly excelling. Suffering isn't necessarily a bad word depending on what it means to you; a little bit of suffering oftentimes brings out the best in people while highlighting their strengths and weaknesses.

How much you want to achieve on your journey depends on how far you're willing to go. Think about what you're going to put into your goals and plans: are you willing to give it your all even when things do not look like they're going the way you want them to? The ability to keep on going even when failure occurs is innate to entrepreneurs who are determined to win. When you're determined, no amount of suffering can stand in your way to success. In fact, it only enhances your experience as you transform hard times into success.

There is Power in Emotional Passion, too.

I want to make a final point here: while I believe the most important key to success is passion—and I most clearly associate that word with the willingness to suffer and endure—if you are also emotionally attached to your product or service, you will reach success even faster.

Here's what I mean. Although some people out there may be emotionally passionate about LED lighting—that was never me. I achieved success because I possessed the kind of passion that made me willing to suffer and willing to endure. But can you imagine with me for a moment how much more successful I would have been had I also been emotionally passionate about LED lighting?

Passion is indeed a key to success. It is the most important key to success as far as I'm concerned. This opinion has been corroborated by the hundreds of guests who have shared their success stories with me on my podcast. Every single one refers to passion as their key to success.

The kind of passion that drives endurance is an indisputable requirement for success. If you aren't willing to endure, you're toast, even if you have a strong emotional connection with your product or service.

Passion is a two-pronged idea. If you have both "prongs," you are sitting in the catbird seat on your way to success. But do not be discouraged from pursuing your business idea if you are not emotionally connected to your business product or service. As long as you're willing to suffer and endure whatever it takes to build that business, you'll be fine. Just know that if you also have that passionate emotional connection, you are on a much faster path to success.

A Final Warning: Beware of the Shiny-Object Syndrome.

So many of the entrepreneurs I know who aren't willing to suffer would prefer to chase shiny objects and look for an easy path to success. That isn't passion. Even when these entrepreneurs are emotionally passionate about the product or service they sell, they don't possess the first key to success: they're unwilling to suffer. They are passive rather than passionate.

If that's who you are as an entrepreneur, I guarantee you will not be successful. The first key to success is always passion. It is always the ability and the willingness to suffer and endure.

If you listen to my podcasts, you will discover that each entrepreneur I interview describes in so many words his or her passion for their endeavor. Some of them are very passionate in terms of the emotional attachment to the thing that they do, the service that they provide, or the product that they sell. But don't be blinded by their emotions. Listen closely, and you will discover how much they were willing to suffer for what they wanted to build—just like Katie Richardson.

For Katie and the other entrepreneurs, their goals aren't a passing fancy. Instead—in many cases—they are formed by an all-consuming desire to build something great. They may or may not have a strong affinity for the product or service they offer, but they are willing to endure and willing to suffer to build something bigger than themselves.

It is in that kind of passion—passion in the true sense of the word is where success begins.

CHAPTER 3

THE RUDOLPH CONUNDRUM

Dr. Dan Young

Director at Wharton-AltFinance, Entrepreneur, TEDx Organizer and Speaker

---

Many of us are familiar with the story, *Rudolph the Red-Nosed Reindeer*. If you're like me, you were first exposed to Rudolph as a child watching Christmas movies. *Rudolph the Red-Nosed Reindeer* is a sensational, stop-motion animated TV special. Every single year, millions gather around the TV to watch the unsung hero. It's become a Christmas tradition for many households. The movie's popularity remained incredibly consistent over the decades. It has been broadcast every year since 1964, making it the longest-running Christmas TV special in history.

Personally, it's still one of my favorite holiday specials to watch—along with *A Christmas Story* and *The Grinch Who Stole Christmas*, of course. I'm struck by Rudolph's perseverance and grit as he leads Santa Claus's sleigh through the thick fog. By doing so, he is able to save Christmas.

As I grew older and became an instructor, assistant professor, and administrator focused on entrepreneurial learning, I realized that many entrepreneurs understand what Rudolph goes through. We want to persevere as he does while we create our entrepreneurial ventures. Who doesn't want to be the underdog who is laughed at, pushed aside, underrated, and eventually rises to the top, leading a team to excellence?

As someone who teaches young people the discipline of entrepreneurship, I found many of them want to attain Rudolph's sense of perseverance and triumph as they journey toward their own business ventures. By the time they get to college, most of these students have identified a problem they wish to solve or an economic opportunity they wish to capture. They come to campus bright-eyed and bushy-tailed, ready to take the world by storm with a new innovation that will change life as we know it.

Many of them have seen movies like *The Social Network, The Boy Who Harnessed the Wind, Steve Jobs,* and other similar films about business achievers, so they realize their ideas will encounter more adversaries than champions. Most of my students want to be the person who gets all the credit for leading a business from a modest start-up to worldwide domination. And perhaps they also envision a nice cinematic moment of being hoisted onto the shoulders of their peers and carried around the classroom while everyone else chants their name.

However, what I know today and share with students is that being an entrepreneur is less about being Rudolph, and much more about being the big guy himself: Santa.

Let's discuss why that is.

Rudolph is the only child of Donner and the appropriately named—if somewhat chauvinistically—Mrs. Donner. We all know that Donner is one of Santa's most prized reindeer. As you may recall, Donner and Mrs. Donner encourage Rudolph to leave the family cave and to make friends with the other reindeer—but only after they cover his bright red nose with mud.

As the movie goes, despite his parents' best efforts, Rudolph's so-called friends eventually make fun of him and won't let him play their reindeer games. After many unusual events and chance meetings,

Rudolph becomes the hero by working with Yukon Cornelius and Hermie the Elf. He rescues his parents and Clarice from the Abominable Snowman and then leads Santa's sleigh through the dense fog that threatened a successful Christmas Eve.

Rudolph clearly has a misunderstood gift. Because no one immediately sees the value of that gift, he is vilified. Only Santa recognizes its value and puts Rudolf at the front of his sleigh.

As entrepreneurs, we tend to hold a vision of being the hero who leads our team through the fog to unbridled success and, in Rudolph's case, the ability to deliver all the toys to all the children. Because of our gift, we are the only ones who can see the finish line. *Yes*, we entrepreneurs want to be lauded by the people we respect and people who counted us out. And *yes*, we want to be celebrated for our accomplishments.

However, Rudolph has many more attributes of a key employee than he has of an entrepreneur. Many employees focus their attention on the expectations of a singular role. They trade hard work for compensation. In the movie, Rudolph's role is definitely singular. He is asked to lead Santa's sleigh because he possesses a unique skill set, there is a need for his role, and he receives a payoff or compensation which, for him, is the opportunity to lead the sleigh team and become a valued member of the group. Rudolf's contribution is a short-term endeavor, however. He is only allowed to lead the others for the singular event of Christmas Eve.

An entrepreneur's expectations are much grander. They have an eye toward scaling their efforts in the long-term by harnessing value and ensuring that skill sets are passed on to others. This is the difference between short-term thinking and long-term thinking as a key component to strategy.

If Rudolph were an entrepreneur, he would have eschewed subsequent trips at the head of the sleigh in lieu of assisting Santa—probably with the help of the industrious Hermie the Elf—to build a long-term solution for future occurrences of dense fog. He would have been more focused on managing the business of toy delivery than the career of head reindeer.

Employees and entrepreneurs differ in other ways too. Many high-skilled employees enjoy being led with specific instructions while entrepreneurs want to lead by developing systems that remove themselves from the equation. Entrepreneurs deftly manage the politics of the workplace while using their own influence to execute plans. Rudolph is not forced to do this; any influence that he gains is a direct result of the positional power that Santa gives him as the one leading the sleigh.

Employees tend to specialize in certain areas while entrepreneurs generalize over entire operations. Rudolph is certainly a specialist; he doesn't make toys and can't manage production. In fact, he spends a majority of his time in the movie wooing Clarice or running from the Abominable Snowman. He is ill-equipped to oversee the entire Christmas operation.

I submit that, for several reasons, Santa Claus is more likely the person that we, as entrepreneurs, want to emulate. Let's take a closer look at Santa's entrepreneurial skills.

Talent Mobilizer

First, let's state the obvious: Santa has a great eye for talent. He sees Rudolph with his gleaming nose and realizes that he can accomplish a task that the other reindeer can't. This ability to identify and mobilize talent is a key trait of successful entrepreneurs. Successful entrepreneurs don't want to be Rudolph; they want to find, hire, and train the rest of the organization to follow more Rudolphs to build success.

Laser-Focused on Vision

In terms of power, entrepreneurs tend to ignore politics and do whatever is necessary to get the job done. They are laser-focused on their vision. They are willing to be innovative, creative, and inspiring. This describes Santa Claus perfectly in the movie. While Rudolph is not the first choice to guide the sleigh that night—based on his coworkers' perceptions of him—Santa used Rudolph's unique talent to accomplish his mission.

By putting Rudolph at the head of the sleigh—thus promoting him—Santa takes the risk of alienating other team members as the other reindeer are much older and more seasoned. Santa sees a quality in Rudolph that others are not willing to accept. He realizes his vision can be achieved because of that quality.

Generalist, Not Specialist

Santa is the textbook definition of a generalist as opposed to a specialist. With very little effort, he is able to manage the elves in the warehouse, prepare the reindeer to drive the sleigh, and motivate a disparate group of individuals to work together toward a common goal.

This story takes place before the days of smartphones, TikTok, and Instagram. Most of the characters in Christmas Town aren't able to see the fruits of their annual labor. Nothing distracts them from believing in Santa's vision and his word that all the toys are of high quality and delivered appropriately.

One of the most interesting and heartfelt moments of the movie concerns Rudolph's visit to The Island of Misfit Toys, the place where defective toys that no child wanted would live together in exile. While Rudolph was able to see value in the inhabitants of the Island of Misfit Toys, it was Santa who had the power to pick them up and deliver them to the children who would place value on their distinctive qualities and match them with children who wanted them. Matching the Misfit toys with children who were looking for those specific qualities was a fine example of another one of Santa's abilities—to see the big picture by understanding target markets and delivering benefits to consumers.

Rule Breakers

Good employees do exactly what their manager asks of them with little hesitation, and they're happy to do jobs that play to their greatest skill sets. Rudolph's "beak that blinks like a blinkin' beacon"—Donner's description of Rudolf's nose—certainly qualifies as a skill set. Rudolf is quick to follow Santa's direction and hop to the head of the sleigh to accomplish his task.

Entrepreneurs, however, are known for breaking rules and protocol to get the job done. Santa clearly has no issues with breaking rules. He takes a little-known commodity in Rudolph and entrusts him with arguably the most important job on the planet—delivering toys to all the good girls and boys.

Decisive

Entrepreneurs are decisive to a fault, even under controversial circumstances that might put them at odds with others. As leaders, entrepreneurs often make unpopular decisions, and they stand by those decisions to ensure they attain their vision.

For example, Santa has strict standards that he expects from others in the form of the "naughty list." You are either naughty or nice; there is no other option. Those of us with children know how hard it is to say *no* to them, especially in the face of a full-scale meltdown. While a less decisive leader—and sometimes, a parent—may decide to give all girls and boys a toy to keep the peace, Santa is resolute in his decision to abstain from rewarding little ones who have misbehaved all year.

As entrepreneurs and leaders, we are often in a position where we must downsize our workforce, have critical conversations with employees, or sometimes, demonstrate tough love. Santa recognizes the power of his position. He understands the delicate balance of peace and goodwill toward humans could easily be thrown off-kilter with a generation of spoiled brats. He knows that his decision to deliver a lump of coal rather than a toy to naughty boys and girls will probably create issues with their parents. However, he is willing to endure the short-term maelstrom of vitriol and outrage for the betterment of society. When these children recognize how serious Santa is about good behavior, they will hopefully modify their actions and move from the naughty to nice list, increasing societal good for everyone.

Adaptive

Santa shows how adaptive he can be, which is a critical skill for entrepreneurs. When the fog rolls in on Christmas Eve, he is momentarily overcome by the concern that Christmas must be cancelled. However, after seeing Rudolph's nose, he pivots, effectively adapting to the new condition: the fog.

Fear is the primary reason many people are unable to fully embrace the law of adaptation. Many tend to overanalyze circumstances which may lead to "analysis paralysis." They are unable to move forward because they're faced with such a wide range of situational variables. However, Santa is decidedly proactive. He does not let his fear of Rudolph's youth or inexperience take over.

Many times, two reasons keep entrepreneurs from being successful: the first is a lack of trust; the second, a lack of discipline. As an entrepreneurial leader, Santa trusts Rudolph to take on the fog challenge and motivates him to do so. Santa clearly understands that Rudolph might fail in his effort, but he is also aware that *not* trying would guarantee failure. By putting Rudolph front and center, Santa trusts him to struggle through the climb and work through the challenges on his own. It takes discipline on Santa's part to bestow this responsibility on Rudolf and let him fly with it, but it's a crucial step for Rudolph's growth, encouraging him to build confidence and grit.

As the entrepreneurial leader, Santa leads from the back. He trusts his team has the necessary drive to pull the sleigh while he steers it and provides the familiar encouragement, "Up, up, up and away!"

Logistics and Work Culture

Operationally, Santa is second to none. He maintains a strong work culture, and he has mastered logistics at a level that would make someone like Henry Ford or even Jeff Bezos jealous. He has created a wonderful production line system that allows the elves to deftly perform the same tasks repeatedly while producing all the toys in the world. Consistency and replication of activity allows the elves to become specialists and experts in specific tasks, increasing their ability to understand their work and provide feedback on better practices.

Santa motivates the elves so well that they constantly sing, dance, and take care of business without needing him to be present all of the time. He does not have to watch over the elves. Instead, he uses floor managers to observe the processes and make quick corrections as necessary to keep everyone on task. This approach frees up time for Santa to scale high-level strategy and, of course, spend more time with Mrs. Claus.

Work-Life Balance

One of the movie's subtle dynamics concerns the relationship between Santa and Mrs. Claus. They are obviously able to communicate effectively, support each other, and maintain a great work-life balance. Each person in the marriage has their own role. Santa manages and leads the toy operation while Mrs. Claus supervises the home front. They demonstrate the ability to speak to each other in a loving fashion and work through their problems.

Sadly, many entrepreneurs are so bogged down with work that they forget to maintain loving banter with their spouse or significant other. As *Rudolph the Red-Nosed Reindeer* shows, Santa sets aside time to engage with Mrs. Claus in a respectful and loving way.

Employee Relations

More kudos to Santa and his entrepreneurial abilities for his eye toward employee relations. Santa clearly has a new star in Rudolph, but he also has several other important roles played by Dasher, Dancer, Prancer, Vixen, Comet, Cupid, Donner, and Blitzen. Ensuring the talent can work with one another is a key facet of effective leadership.

Many of these reindeer—including Rudolph's own father—doubt Rudolph's potential for success. Santa demonstrates his entrepreneurial leadership by motivating them to work together with Rudolph so they can deliver all the toys to all the good little girls and boys in the world.

Ability to Scale

Entrepreneurs strive for scalability. In the case of Santa Claus's sleigh, there is one line of business: toy delivery. That business means working effectively with Rudolph and the other reindeer to drive that sleigh every Christmas Eve.

As an entrepreneur, imagine scaling that business to include 10 of those sleighs. Now 100. Now 1,000! Each sleigh would need their own Rudolph complete with grit, determination, and that specific skill set. As the business scales, more Rudolphs become necessary. With 1,000 Rudolphs and 1,000 teams of the other reindeer, success is guaranteed.

More Than a "Special Something"

Modern media promotes the avatar of a courageous entrepreneur. Whether it is Andrew Carnegie, Oprah Winfrey, or Richard Branson, we are presented with entrepreneurs who have that "special something" and can make straw into gold just like Rumpelstiltskin. While special traits certainly propelled these particular individuals to gain initial success, funding, and employees, it does not necessarily lead to long-term business success, at least not the business success that creates billion-dollar valuations. It takes much more than that to truly be an entrepreneur.

To grow each of their businesses to new heights, each of these entrepreneurs eventually had to learn the skills that Santa so deftly wields in *Rudolph the Red-Nosed Reindeer*. Rudolph-style bright noses may get us in the door and get us noticed, but it takes the harder-to-acquire skills of Santa to make a global impact.

It starts with a discerning eye for talent. If an entrepreneur is always the smartest person in the room, the business cannot grow once they leave the meeting. Entrepreneurs must take calculated risks while still pioneering.

Each of these successful CEOs has a compelling and enduring vision that they communicate not only to their workers but to the entire world. These CEOs are well-read in several different areas and not just in the specific skill that made them wealthy. They are able and willing to break the rules of their industry while refusing to budge from their standards. They are highly adaptable. At the same time, they show high degrees of trust and discipline with their decision-making. Like Santa, they do not mind leading from the back when the time calls for it; they understand they are still steering the sleigh. They develop strong relationships and stay loyal to their most trusted lieutenants. They are operationally proficient and understand what drives revenue and adoption with their products and services. They can get diverse groups to work together for a common goal and can scale a business to its greatest value.

These traits of great entrepreneurs have endured throughout time. So, even though Rudolph went down in history, he will never be as important as Santa Claus—because Santa Claus is the greatest entrepreneur of all time.

CHAPTER 4

LET GO OF THE WHEEL

Mark Hayes

Real Estate Investor, Angel Investor, and Entrepreneur

I vividly remember the first time I drove a vehicle. I was just 13 and at the beach with my best friend's family, which included his 16-year-old brother. Without his parent's permission, that 16-year-old let me drive the family minivan. Although it was fun to drive, I quickly learned that operating a vehicle takes serious concentration and control.

Entrepreneurs have similar experiences in their businesses. Starting a business is exciting, but most entrepreneurs want to sit behind the wheel and control every aspect of it. Like driving in heavy traffic, entrepreneurship can be stressful. Driving too many different departments can put growth into a gridlock. We may feel as though we need to "grind" to finish the race, but if we're driving for long hours, we will eventually run out of gas.

Leaders must realize what their time is worth. Only then can they recognize when to let go of the wheel and let someone else drive, freeing up their time to focus on the entrepreneurial journey.

The 10 and 2 Positions

One of the first lessons in driving illustrates where to place hands on the steering wheel for optimal control. I was taught to grip the 10 and 2 positions, referencing 10 a.m. and 2 p.m. on an analog clock.

For the first ten years of my real estate investing career, I gripped my business like I gripped that steering wheel. I wanted control. No one could manage my building renovations better than me. No one could manage my rentals better than me.

To operate my business efficiently, I decided to purchase properties in only one zip code. At the time, I thought that was a smart decision; it would let me check on multiple properties and meet contractors and tenants within a short drive time. I wore many hats to operate a one-man show of flips and rentals. I handled marketing to generate leads and acquire properties. I dealt with bankers to attain financing. I managed hiring for construction projects and oversaw subcontractors. I showed vacant rentals, handled leases, collected rents, and oversaw maintenance. I managed buy-and-sell transactions while coordinating with title companies, real estate agents, appraisers, and home inspectors. With zero previous bookkeeping experience under my belt, I learned QuickBooks and handled bill payments, contractor payments, and reconciling multiple accounts. I also handled all administrative duties during a decade of transitioning from mostly paper and some digital record-keeping to everything in digital format.

By the end of 2012, in addition to running my business, I was the general contractor for building my personal home while my wife was pregnant with our fourth child, due in July 2013. (This must have been the year I started balding!)

In January of 2013, I attended the seminar "How to Run a Business Like a Business." The seminar was led by Robyn Thompson, an active real estate investor and an expert in rehabbing homes to make large profits. The first point she made in the class was to avoid minimum wage activities, or MWAs.

After the first break of the all-day class, I went up to Ms. Thompson and explained I could only handle a couple of construction projects at a time.

"What's your advice on how to grow?" I asked.

"You need to hire an assistant," she said.

My heart skipped a beat. "But no one else can do things as well as I can!"

"That's probably true," she replied, "but if someone can do the job at least 80% as good as you can, it will free up your time to do something else."

Although I didn't want to take my hands off 10 and 2, by the end of the class, I was beginning to realize my desire for control was stifling my growth and my income.

The following week, after meeting a plumber at one of my houses, I got a call from the painter working up the street on another home.

"We need the water turned on to keep working," he said.

To make sure the painter and his crew wouldn't leave, I would have to drive to my office, pick up the water key, go to the property to turn on the water, and return to my office where I planned to spend the afternoon on my computer. This task would take about 30 minutes.

After hanging up, I remembered Robyn's advice: avoid the MWAs.

I called the plumber, who carried a key on his truck, and asked if he'd mind driving up the street to turn on the water for the painters.

He agreed.

A 30-second phone call saved me 30 minutes.

What's Your Time Worth?

Calculating what your time is worth is easy. Divide your gross income goal for the year by the number of weeks you plan to work. Divide the quotient by the number of hours you want to work per week. Here is an example:

$1,000,000 ÷ 48 weeks = $20,833.33 per week

$20,833.33 ÷ 30 hours = $694.44 per hour

If you feel you are not worth your calculated wage, it will reflect in a lower income. A rule of thumb is this: if you have a task or job that you can hire someone to do for less than your projected hour rate of $694 per hour, then hire someone. To better optimize your time, constantly evaluate whether the tasks and duties you're undertaking personally are valued at your calculated rate.

Increase by Letting Go

In 2013, I hired a full-time office manager to assist with administration, property management, and bookkeeping. I also hired a general contractor for my construction projects. This freed up my time to acquire more deals, secure additional financing, and handle more projects. From 2012 to 2013, my income increased 38%. From 2013 to 2014, my income increased 109%.

Enough said.

In early 2017, my office manager informed me she was leaving to pursue her own bookkeeping business. I faced another decision and the questions that came with it. What was my time worth? Should I hire and train another full-time office manager? Or hire a professional property management company and a part-time office manager?

I hired a property management company for my rentals, and that turned out to be the second-best decision of my business career. During this transition, I realized I was not charging the current market value for rentals. As vacancies occurred, the property manager corrected the situation by raising the rents, effectively offsetting the management fee.

But even better, he took care of maintenance, leasing, collecting rent, and other time-consuming tasks associated with property management so I could focus elsewhere. This also expanded my ability to invest in areas beyond one zip code—something I had originally believed would help me save time. Having a property manager created a paradigm shift to that thinking. I now have rental properties in three different cities and spend maybe one hour per week on my rental portfolio.

Managing Rush Hour

Nashville has three interstates running through the city center. When I attended Vanderbilt University, two and sometimes three other guys and I volunteered to coach soccer for inner-city kids at the Martha O'Bryan Center. Once a week around 4:30 p.m., spring and fall, we would take the chaotic drive through the city center on I-40 East, which intersects with two other interstates. That meant changing three lanes of traffic and crossing the Silliman Evans Bridge to East Nashville. The drive was always nerve-wracking. Even just reading the directions from Vanderbilt University to the Martha O'Bryan Center was stressful!

Just as driving down a chaotic interstate can create stress, a chaotic business schedule can have the same result. But with the right attention and planning, it doesn't have to be that way.

Organize Tasks

Organizing tasks to maximize time is crucial. Through his course, The Business Accelerator, Jason Duncan—another author contributing to this book—taught me how to better organize my to-do list. He referred to existing tasks as "open cycles" and divided them into three categories: To do now, to do in one week or less, and to do long-term or involve others. Dividing tasks into these categories creates better organization and more efficient completion. He also taught me to schedule my week in ten blocks and avoid distractions during those times. I highly recommend Jason's courses.

Determine Urgency and Importance

Another great method to manage time comes from Stephen Covey's book, *Seven Habits of Highly Effective People*. In this book, first published in 1989 with several subsequent editions, Covey divides task urgency and importance into four quadrants:

- Quadrant 1: Urgent and important
- Quadrant 2: Not urgent but important
- Quadrant 3: Urgent but not important
- Quadrant 4: Not urgent and not important

As you can see, Covey explains that important tasks are not necessarily urgent, and urgent tasks are not necessarily important. Therefore, we need to spend most of our time in Quadrant 2: "not urgent but important" so we can invest time into the tasks that will best help us achieve our goals.

Focus on the Here and Now

With the advancement of technology and today's busy pace, attention is pulled in many directions. Have you ever unlocked your smartphone to send someone a text or email only to find an alert, notification, or another text that grabs your attention? After reading through all those distractions, it's easy to forget why you looked at your phone in the first place.

Most of us tend to focus a lot of our time on the past, which causes guilt or regret—even though we are unable to change past circumstances. We also spend a lot of time speculating on future events that may never happen, causing worry. In fact, we spend only 8% of our time focusing on activities that are important, the kind that can change current experiences. And that's where we should place most of our focus.

In 2012, I purchased a historic home to renovate and sell. It was built in 1915 and had wood-stained trim and irreplaceable fireplace mantels. Due to the home's small footprint, I invited a designer to plan for an addition on the back. I viewed the process of seamlessly incorporating the old with the new as my most prized project to date.

I went into the project knowing the floors of the home needed leveling, but I hadn't realized the existing home would need new footings and a new foundation. This complicated and expensive proposition required the home to be raised on large timbers spanning from the front to the back of the structure. For a few weeks, I woke up in the middle of every night, worrying about possible issues.

None of these issues arose. I lost a lot of sleep because I was engrossed on the future instead of the present.

Delegating to the Right People

Looking back, as a young professional influenced by hard-working parents, I did not want to let pride make me feel as though any job was below me, so I felt obligated to do everything. However, by doing tasks that others could do for me, I robbed others of a potential wage, stifled their growth, and forced myself to work harder—and longer—than I should.

When I was hiring an office manager, one candidate stated on her resume, "I work smarter, not harder."

I hired her. It reminded me of an experience I'd had the summer before my senior year in college, I had worked at a small engineering firm as a technician. My job involved visiting construction sites, working in the testing laboratory at the office, and writing reports. Other staff included experienced technicians, two engineers, an administrative assistant, and an office manager. The other staff would ridicule the office manager for having an easy job and accuse him of not working. He would walk around the office sipping from his coffee mug and conversing with the other staff. With one year left in college, knowing I would work for a similar firm after completing my degree, I envied him. Years later, I realized that he had been paid to think. He was not "working hard" but "working smart," just like the office manager I eventually hired.

Delegation takes trust. It can be easy to make decisions based on past experiences. However, just because you made one "bad hire" doesn't mean the next employee will turn out the same. In the construction business, many contractors have told me they can't hire "good people" so they end up doing the work themselves. This behavior ensures they become prisoners to their businesses. It shatters their chances of growth, and most likely results in lost clients.

At the end of the day, most business owners who lack trust wind up building a job rather than a business. They work long hours and sometimes don't pay themselves. Although they are simply trading hours for dollars, restricted to the conditions that led them to quit their jobs and start their own business in the first place. They struggle to keep their heads above water, which leaves no time to expand the business.

Expanding the business means hiring employees to do some of the tasks, especially those that are worth less than the value of your time. You might have heard the phrase, "Hire slow, fire fast." Creating steps for hiring can help to ensure employees are a good fit with the company. For example, create an application form with your own questions instead of reviewing resumes. Conduct a brief phone interview before deciding if a face-to-face interview is warranted. Organize a culture check by allowing your team members to spend time with the candidate.

There are other ways to get people on your team too. Consider a virtual assistant. They can be an effective way to run a business and give people in countries like the Philippines, where many speak English well, an opportunity to work at a wage fair to them. Or trade mentorship for time with interns. An eager intern who wants to learn hands-on entrepreneurship makes a great personal assistant. The training and experience they receive is worth the cost of business school tuition, but some entrepreneurs I know also pay a small wage to their interns.

Author Jim Collins studies the importance of hiring the right people in his book, *Good to Great*. On his website, he describes its content:

"First Who, Then What—get the right people on the bus"—is a concept developed in the book, *Good to Great*. Those who build great organizations make sure they have the right people on the bus and the right people in the key seats before they figure out where to drive the bus. They always think first about who and then about what. When facing chaos and uncertainty, and you cannot possibly predict what's coming around the corner, your best "strategy" is to have a busload of people who can adapt to and perform brilliantly no matter what comes next. Great vision without great people is irrelevant.

As a business leader, organizing open cycles, managing time in terms of urgency and importance, being present, and delegating tasks to others are key. These steps let you focus on working ON the business, instead of IN the business. With some careful planning and attention, you can shift the nature of your drive. Would you rather travel through crazy rush hour traffic or take a more peaceful, scenic drive? Even if you can't completely alter your route, you can find ways to manage the chaos.

Choose the Right Vehicle for the Job

Always keep your eyes open for the right vehicle for the job to create more efficiency.

When I was still rehabbing homes early in my career, I felt the need to own a pickup truck. I went from a small four-door Saturn to a Chevy S-10 to a Toyota Tacoma. Driving a truck made me feel like a true American, especially in the South. Trucks can be loud and ride rough. Similar to my original idea that buying property in only one zip code was efficient, I thought owning a truck was efficient. Owning a truck came with a risk, however. It gave me a reason to pick up supplies and haul items away from my project sites. In other words, it tempted me to perform MWAs.

On a personal note, when friends and family found out I had a truck, the phone calls of favors to borrow my vehicle or help move furniture came rolling in. I enjoy helping friends and family, but if you have ever owned a truck, you know what I am talking about. "Work" is in a truck's definition.

Once my wife and I began to have kids, we sold the truck. It wasn't suitable transportation. Without the truck, I could no longer haul supplies, tools, or trash. I paid someone else to do it and was happy to let that go.

Rethink Your Approach

When it comes to success, "more" is usually not the answer. In fact, as we progress, "less" may be the key to reaching our fullest potential. The first year I began funding other real estate investors' projects with bridge loans, the average loan was approximately $110,000. After two or three years, I funded fewer loans, but the average loan was higher, around $160,000. As a result, I spent less time in this business while the revenue remained the same or better.

Find the Right Partners

Have you ever been introduced to someone with whom you could potentially build a relationship that would benefit you both financially? Instead of taking the time to make a big leap and call them to explore the idea, you find yourself caught up in busy work. We are prone to taking a lot of small actions rather than larger ones because our mindset has been trained around scarcity and survival. People who accomplish large actions think in terms of abundance. They thrive. Although it may at first feel unnatural to take big actions or large leaps of faith, that feeling will quickly vanish when results appear.

Block Your Time Wisely

Most of us are more productive during a certain block of time. If you don't already know what your most productive time is, figure it out. Schedule work that requires concentrated focus during that time, or work on a series of similar tasks for greater productivity.

Working for the sake of checking it off a list moves you further away from your goal. If you act with precision and speed, you are sure to get good results fitting to the actions. However, a reluctant or careless approach can lead to poor execution, negating the potential for good outcomes. Working all year without getting further ahead leads to frustration.

Reduce Actions, Not Effort

If you strive to have a broad, positive impact in the world, then it is imperative to start reducing the number of actions you take. You do not need to reduce efforts. Instead, focus on fewer, larger, and more strategic actions. These larger actions will produce greater results. They're key to accomplishing more than you ever thought possible.

To be successful as a business leader, you must design and guide the vision and mission of your business. Although this may seem simple enough, many businesses fail within the first couple of years because they fail to plan. As the founder of your business, you have three primary roles to plan for.

The first is to gain clarity of vision for the company's future and to identify what goals and practices need to be implemented to accomplish those intentions.

The second is to communicate your vision clearly to everyone on your team. Provide them with the directives they need to meet their goals and let them know what procedures are necessary to accomplish the vision. To accomplish set objectives and implement the systems necessary to get the company running smoothly and efficiently, be sure to delegate. Keeping your head down and working diligently to implement the necessary action steps all by yourself takes your eyes off the road. You won't be able to see where the company is going.

The third and most important role of the founder is to focus on building your assets. Most business owners are dedicated to running successful companies. However, they fail to take the steps necessary to create valuable assets. Assets include sub-products and services, and exclusive marketing solutions, software or other branded technology that can be sold to competitors. Owning real estate is also a great method to build the company's value.

Most people are taught to work hard in school, make good grades, and graduate from college to get a "good" job. Entrepreneurs and business leaders choose different vehicles. They rethink the typical approach to making a living by finding the right partners, blocking their time wisely, and reducing their actions rather than their efforts. These steps are key to greater success.

Cruise Control

With 20-plus years of entrepreneurship under my belt, I've found that the road I travel is never mundane. The journey brings lots of opportunities to learn about other people's journeys, and at the same time, build solid relationships for the ride.

Using cruise control so I can focus on planning the route brings flexibility and freedom. My business is stronger. I have the resources I need to give back financially and increase my circle of influence. Most importantly, I have control over my time—something that benefits my personal life as well. With four kids so close together in age, my wife and I constantly juggle school events and other activities. Entrepreneurship allows me to shift my schedule as needed to make sure they are all covered.

Time is the most valuable asset. You'll find more of it if you're willing to let go of the wheel.

CHAPTER 5

THE PURPOSE & POWER OF MENTORSHIP

Bobby Dunaway

Book Publisher, Entrepreneur, and CEO of Indigo River Publishing

Mentorship lies at the root of effective leadership. When that root is nurtured, the aspirations of great leaders flourish—and so do the lives of those who cross their paths. However, despite its potential rewards, mentorship requires the fertilizer of time and energy to be successful. Many entrepreneurs struggle to see the benefits of using their precious resources for mentoring others. Yet, there is so much to be gained! Consider a brief story that illustrates this point.

Matthew and Jesse were twin brothers from a wealthy family. They received a considerable inheritance as adults. While Matthew's fortune increased exponentially, Jesse struggled to match his impressive results. Although both were astute businesspeople, they had different approaches to business. While Jesse, who was more calculating, focused on time and efficiency, Matthew exuded warmth and generosity with his wealth and time.

Jesse approached Matthew to discover how he could thrive, too. As the brothers conversed on one of their factory floors, Jesse asked,

"How can you be so prosperous when you give away so much money and time?"

Matthew reached into a nearby barrel full of seed and then clenched his fist tightly. When he drew his hand back and opened it, only a sparse number of seeds lay in his palm. "This is how you're operating now."

Then Matthew reached into the barrel again, this time with an open hand, and scooped out a heaping pile of seeds. "You can hold onto more with an open hand than a clenched and grasping fist," he explained.

By sharing this point with Jesse, Matthew did more than provide a business tip. He engaged in mentoring by offering a practical life lesson, a gift that reflected sincere personal interest.

But what is mentoring, really?

Mentorship: Fundamental to Life and Business

Mentoring, at its core, is personalized instruction. Before the age of public schooling, affluent families often hired a private tutor to educate their children and prepare them for a career. Serving as a tutor was a valued and trusted role.

We derive the modern use of the word mentorship from the role of tutor and a classical story. In his novel, *The Adventures of Telemachus, Son of Ulysses*, a sequel to Homer's Greek epic poem, *The Odyssey*, François Fénelon recounts the exploits of Telemachus. Telemachus is guided and instructed by his tutor, named Mentor, who happens to be the goddess of wisdom in disguise, Athena. With Athena's guidance, Telemachus embarks on a quest to learn more about his father, who left when he was still an infant. Through that mentorship, Telemachus learns to overcome adversity and challenge, becoming a hero in his own right.

As Matthew and Mentor illustrate, mentorship is more than simply training someone with a few work skills or bestowing nuggets of wisdom. It involves close personal instruction that equips another individual to attain greatness and then go on to influence others. Anyone who has ever made an indelible mark on the world benefitted from a mentor's guidance at some point in their past. These bellwethers went on to become mentors themselves.

This cycle of mentorship is the source of all significant achievements. If you want to make an impact, you must become an effective mentor. Embarking on that quest raises a few questions about mentorship:

What are its core principles?

What forms can mentorship take?

What type of mentor are you?

The rest of this chapter will help you discover the fundamentals of mentorship and how to put them into practice.

Six Core Principles of Successful Mentorship

Use the following six principles to become a mentor or improve your current mentoring activities.

1. Prepare Yourself Mentally and Emotionally

Successful mentorship demands that you focus more on building character than developing head knowledge. You must accept the challenge of molding another human mind, the most precious and potent resource in the world. Never take such a privilege lightly.

Such preparation also requires a level of humility. When most of us assume a position of leadership, it's easy to become overconfident. However, the best teachers are eternal learners, and you must accept that you will make mistakes as you mentor. Your mentee may even call you out on some errors. Acknowledge your flaws and use each as a teachable experience.

Never lose your desire to grow as an individual and as a leader. Create an action plan to implement what you learn. Begin by setting tangible benchmarks and goals. For example, you can focus on honing one particular aspect of mentoring every week. When you've covered everything, start over again. Repetition is crucial.

Even more vital than fortifying your mind is preparing your heart. Above all, feel sincere concern for those whom you mentor. Genuine interest and a strong relationship are more motivating than words and direction.

Your first foray into mentorship usually requires accepting the challenge of working with a diamond in the rough, discovering the potential in someone that others may have missed. As you mold and refine grateful mentees, their successes impact you as well. For example, their achievements might spark a good buzz around your business that attracts high-quality employees. A mentee's growth might mean being able to trust them with responsibility for some of your tasks so that you can focus on bigger-picture objectives.

2. Create a Genuine Connection

The danger of superficial mentorship is common in professional settings where leaders can impose mentorship on employees or interns. However, the most productive mentor-mentee relationships are not one-sided. The system works best when both the mentor and mentee are willing participants. Many organizations claim to be a "family" but fail to create warm bonds. Selecting job candidates wisely and making the expectation of mentorship evident during the hiring process eliminates incompatibility. Build a unit founded on fostering the human spirit and uplifting your team, not just attracting clients.

All relationships take time and require patience. From the moment your mentoring program begins, engender goodwill and a personal connection with your mentees. You may be excited to flood your new student with your vast stores of information. However, people enjoy drinking out of a gentle fountain but find little refreshment from the blast of a firehose, so pour out your wisdom gradually at first. Focus on understanding your mentee rather than putting them into a box of preconceived notions. Discern each other's communication styles and adapt. As you prioritize the bond, teaching opportunities will naturally arise.

3. Building Expectations

Never lose sight of your goal to help your mentee progress professionally. When collaborating with an employee, you can easily set clear benchmarks related to performance. However, when you mentor as a volunteer or trade your mentorship for someone's time and skills, you might struggle to hold yourself accountable. To avoid that difficulty, define from the start what you will offer the mentee and what you expect in return. Timely milestones determine if the relationship is yielding results. Without clear goals and the sensation of forward movement, the relationship will fizzle out.

Clear expectations also set the stage for creating fair exchange, for ensuring the mentor and mentee each benefit from the relationship. For example, if you're starting a new business, you may not have the capital to hire freelancers or employees. Offering to take a promising individual under your wing in exchange for their work as an assistant can help your business take root while offering invaluable experience to your mentee.

Good mentees can often be found through formal college internships, but don't limit yourself to that format. Consider locating a few different mentees for different duties. You might find a student who can serve as a personal assistant and perform tasks like taking calls, sending emails, and creating social media campaigns. Another mentee could be a driver, while another might serve as a "gofer" taking care of time-consuming odds and ends. If each of these mentees provide you with 10 to 15 hours of service per week, you gain the power of human capital. You'll have the equivalent of a full-time assistant through a team of volunteers who provide labor in exchange for guidance, leaving you with more time to do the big-picture work.

Include your mentees in team meetings and introduce them to professional circles. Also, dedicate a set time daily to provide advice and feedback. This attention will facilitate their professional growth.

Promising individuals often take advantage of working for free to break into an industry. This is most common in artistic fields, where people have to hone their talents individually and perform to any available crowd for free. Steven Spielberg is a brilliant example of mentorship, as is Warren Buffett. Both men were willing to work for free and apprentice to others to prove themselves and make headway in their respective industries.

Unsurprisingly, Spielberg became an influential mentor, offering guidance to fellow filmmaker J.J. Abrams. This chain of mentorship is now responsible for over $23 billion in worldwide box office earnings—nearly $16 billion from Spielberg and over $7 billion from Abrams.

A caution here: do not take advantage of the situation or view it as free labor. The relationship must yield definite opportunities for the mentee and be one of fair exchange.

Also, do not presume the student will benefit through sheer osmosis and association. Promises of possibilities that never materialize will earn you a reputation as untrustworthy. Then your access to high-quality mentees with valuable human capital will evaporate.

Create clear expectations for both of you, and your mentoring will offer an abundance of benefits.

4. Active Listening and Providing Actionable Feedback

Avoid the error of making assumptions and providing advice too quickly. Humans are complex and sometimes chaotic beings. Determining how to assist anyone requires a keen ear. For good reason, in psychiatry—a form of mentorship—the practitioner is one who listens and asks questions that prompt self-discovery.

Even when you think you've heard enough about a situation or scenario, listen some more. Although this can be difficult when a mentee tends to talk too much or gets easily sidetracked, using finely tuned questions can help you get to the heart of a matter. Don't provide direction until you truly reach the crux of an issue. Sometimes, that direction will include actionable instruction with measurable benchmarks.

More often, you must teach principles that can serve any area of life or business. A list of dos and don'ts only goes so far, but principles carry a student much further. For example, say you provide a list of rules to your mentee for interacting with clients. Because technology and commerce continually change, rules need continual adjustment too. Your mentee will likely return to you repeatedly for guidance. However, should you teach your mentee the principle of offering a fair exchange with partners and clients—and demonstrate how to create that kind of relationship—your mentee will acquire the skill too. They'll learn how to respond in unique scenarios without needing that changing list of rules for guidance.

5. Teaching with Storytelling

Who can forget Aesop's fables of the tortoise and the hare or the lion and the mouse? These simple stories bring life to the universal truths that "slow and steady wins the race" and "a kindness is never wasted."

Fight the temptation to lecture and expound endlessly about abstract concepts without using real-life examples or word pictures. The mind captures ideas best when expressed in illustrations or object lessons. The more you tailor those lessons to the student's experience, the greater impact they will have. Creating a pithy narrative may not be intuitive for you, but with practice, you can master the skill.

6. Commendation and Empathy

The business world can be cold and merciless. You can't be afraid to offer straight talk and counsel to your mentee when necessary, or they will never grow. Still, this counsel must come from a place of empathy, even when giving "tough love."

To this end, you can hardly provide too much commendation. However, praise is ineffective if it is insincere. Some instructors adopt a "sandwich" approach when they have to correct students by offering a compliment, correction, then a final piece of commendation. This method only works when each layer of the sandwich is nutritious. Whatever you share must be sincere and actionable.

The praise cannot be a generic "attagirl" or "attaboy" or "good job." Isolate what was most impressive so the student can repeat what works. Then highlight one or two items to give attention to for improvement. Conclude with sincere appreciation for the effort. This tactic requires patience and attention, but it can work wonders with an eager mentee.

Apply the preceding core principles, and your mentoring will be an overwhelming success. Now consider five formats for mentoring you can use.

Five Effective Approaches to Mentoring

Using a variety of approaches to instruction is most effective because human minds love novelty and activity. Thus, you should employ a variety of teaching and mentoring methods and formats. Lean most heavily into the formats that work for you and your mentees but be adaptable. Don't be afraid to try something new.

1. One-on-One

One-on-one training is the quintessential mentoring format. Since your time is limited, reserve this method for your most promising mentees. Personal mentoring is a must for those with exceptional abilities and potential. These eager students require dedicated attention, or you will lose them to someone who will satisfy their thirst for personal growth.

The top advantage of one-on-one mentoring is its capability to build a strong, lifelong attachment. It also permits the mentee to shadow you and see you in action.

2. Group-Based

Group-based mentoring is just as essential as one-on-one. Here, you get to see how your mentees interact with each other and display their interpersonal skills.

Successfully mentoring on a group basis is challenging to do effectively. For instance, most people realize that large schoolroom classes become unwieldy for even the best teachers. So, restrict the size of your group-based mentoring sessions to the number of people you can competently assist. However, be sure not to let gifted yet quiet individuals shrink into the background.

Group-based mentoring can save time and multiply your efforts because mentees work together, train each other, and offer additional accountability through peer-based mentoring.

3. Peer-Based

All of us should take advantage of peer-based mentoring throughout our lifetimes. There is nothing like sharing knowledge and experience with those who understand our position. We need to encourage our mentees to do the same. Seize upon peer-based mentoring through mastermind groups and networking. Rely on it more as you rise through professional ranks and have fewer superiors in wealth and experience.

A fair exchange of benefits is crucial in peer-based mentoring since participants are professional equals. Encourage your mentees to find opportunities to practice peer-based mentoring, too, and use your own example to show how peer-based mentoring will be a perpetual resource of education.

4. Reverse

The truly brilliant mind is willing to learn new things from anyone—even a small child. One way to confirm that your mentees will become outstanding mentors themselves is to allow them to teach you.

Young people, in particular, have the curiosity and energy to learn new skills. They quickly adopt technological advancements and innovations. Don't be afraid to learn from them and pick up new skills. This gives you a chance to see how well they can instruct others—and it gives them practice in doing so.

You will not lose the respect of your pupils by being open to learning new ideas. Your continued desire for knowledge and advancement will stir appreciation and inspire their own enthusiasm for growth.

5. Secret

When you become a truly great mentor, others around you will imitate your actions without your knowledge. In other words, you will become a secret mentor to many—including your peers.

The best way to become an outstanding mentor is to model exemplary behavior now, even if you have no mentee under your tutelage. Just as you should dress for the job you want, not the one you have, you should practice the behavior of a thought leader now, and eventually you will attract exceptional mentees.

Use these tips to become a top-tier mentor. As you discover other mentoring formats, find ways to blend them with the above methods.

Six Mentoring Personalities

Understanding your own personality and strengths is essential to creating a successful mentor-mentee relationship. Matthew Reeves, CEO of the Together Software workplace mentorship platform, identifies at least eight mentorship styles based on a person's character.

I've adapted his information here and distilled them into six personalities. Consider which one you might be or what blend of these traits you have. Lean into your strengths and compensate for weaknesses to be effective.

1. Protector

A mentor who focuses on creating a safe space is a protector. Protectors are best suited for mentees who are at the beginning of their professional journey. They may be raw from a difficult life, such as a poverty-stricken upbringing or abusive relationships, or from the impact of another mentor who took advantage of them.

A protector has to work against the tendency to be overly protective or become an enabler. The highest form of mentorship turns mentees into self-sufficient leaders and mentors themselves. A protector must learn to take on other mentorship roles and graduate the mentee to greater self-reliance, or else they will create a dependency that stunts the mentee's growth.

2. Sponsor

The sponsor is a cheerleader who advocates for the mentee and provides connections through their status or network. No one advances professionally solely on ability. That ability needs to attract people in the right positions who can aid an individual's career. Sponsors best serve gifted individuals who have not gained the skills to sell themselves and need a boost to progress professionally and meet their full potential.

However, the sponsor can fall into the trap of providing too much help. This type of mentor should encourage the mentee to recognize their own value and to use their own position to uplift others.

3. Advisor

An advisor fits the traditional concept of a mentor. Advisors will typically be on the same career path as their mentees, but this does not have to be the case.

Advisors tend to prefer instructing in a formal manner. They often need to focus on improving listening skills and empathy while fighting the temptation to solve every problem or give advice. They should also allow the mentee to make some mistakes and not be overly critical of errors.

4. Clarifier

The clarifier works well with mentees who are self-directed and only need a subtle push in the right direction. This is strictly an organizational mentor who helps a mentee learn the ropes. Since clarifiers don't have to do as much handholding, mistakes on the part of the mentor are rarer. Working as a clarifier can be a great role for someone who is just beginning to mentor.

However, the clarifier must be careful not to be too hands-off. Clarifiers must discern when to support a mentee actively when additional help is needed.

5. Challenger

Challengers work best with advanced mentees who are already professionals moving well along in their field. Challengers deliver the hard facts, and the mentees they work with should be able to take that counsel and even offer spirited pushback.

Challengers need to temper their tough love and be mindful of being too hard-edged. This type of mentor suits high-performing executives who have left any thin-skinned traits behind.

6. Coach

Coaches are nearly perfect mentors for any situation. They are excellent listeners who encourage and commend others liberally. This would be the apex of mentorship, where a leader can identify the traits of a mentee and guide them toward problem-solving effectively.

Wherever your talents lie, fine-tune them to become a premier mentor. Determine how you can adapt the strengths of other mentor types and work to ascend to the level of the Coach.

Inspiring Examples of Mentorship

Classical Greek society lays a substantial foundation for modern education and culture, especially through a specific trio of mentoring connections. The conqueror, Alexander the Great, learned at the feet of Aristotle, a student of Plato, who himself learned from Socrates.

Interestingly, *The Adventures of Telemachus, Son of Ulysses*, which has Greek roots through Homer's *Odyssey*, was reportedly a favorite of Thomas Jefferson, the third American President and an early proponent of public education. Unsurprisingly, Jefferson himself benefitted from mentorship. As a law student, he met George Wythe, who became his mentor in matters of politics, law, and culture.

Wythe became one of the signers of the Declaration of Independence, assisted in creating the Virginia Constitution, and served as a professor of law and policy at the College of William and Mary for a decade. He died in 1806, living long enough to see Jefferson assume the Presidency and guide the new nation toward its global dominance.

Another notable example of embracing and surpassing the assistance of a mentor is Ada Lovelace. Although she may not have a direct connection to classical Greece, we owe our modern computers to her genius and foresight—and perhaps to those of her mother. Lovelace's mother encouraged her to pursue her gifts in mathematics and science. Lovelace eventually connected with Charles Babbage and received training from him. Together, they laid the foundation for what modern computing could accomplish. We owe our digital age to Lovelace and the mentors who aided her.

A more modern example of outstanding mentorship is Oprah Winfrey, who oversees an empire worth billions. She relied on the advice and guidance of poet Maya Angelou to maintain her balance and commitment to her dreams.

If such famous figures and creative forces appreciate the value of mentorship, you must recognize the power of mentorship in your own life. Embrace it as a fundamental tenet of how you operate, not as a chore to complete.

Avoid the Temptation to Neglect Mentorship

A final caution is necessary. Like other long-term investments, it's easy to put off mentorship. Entrepreneurs usually scramble to manage day-to-day operations. Many times, a leader may simply handle a task themself rather than take the time to mentor and train another person.

However, this cuts short the life of your organization and your dreams. Who will handle those smaller details when you need to attend to larger issues? Who will carry on your legacy when you're gone? You can only ensure enduring influence by mentoring others.

The situation is similar to maintaining a vehicle. You refuel your car because the effect of not doing so is immediate. Without gas, the vehicle won't run. However, you can delay other maintenance items, such as an oil or tire change, without immediate harm. Eventually, though, you cut short the life of your vehicle because you neglected maintenance with long-term benefits.

So, when running your organization, don't neglect to "change the oil!" Mentoring is part of the maintenance and lubrication that gives your entrepreneurial efforts sustained success.

Enjoy a Lifetime of Mentoring

Mentorship is foundational for our success as a human society in business and relationships. As a leader, you must create systems of mentorship in your own organization and create a legacy of mentors to follow you.

Become an effective mentor through empathy, listening, clear expectation, and fair exchange. Determine the type of mentor you are, how your mentee absorbs information, and the forms of mentoring that work best. When you accept and perfect your role as a mentor, you will embrace what it means to be a true leader and enhance your impact as an entrepreneurship.

CHAPTER 6

YOUR ENTREPRENEURIAL STYLE & WHY IT MATTERS

By Ellen Moran

Coach, Talent, and Culture Strategist,

Specialist in the Simplexity Innovation Process

I **only had 20 minutes** to introduce myself and my coaching approach to a start-up CEO who needed help with his leadership team. It was important to quickly size up the specific challenges he faced and offer a potential solution that made sense to him and gave him enough confidence to schedule a follow-up conversation.

Fred, a successful serial entrepreneur, had lately sensed conflict among key members of his team. This detracted conflict from what they needed to be doing: quickly developing the infrastructure required to meet pent-up client demand for their services. Seemingly petty sniping about various issues could really hurt their ability to build out and scale the offering. The negative dynamic had to be nipped in the bud.

Fred described his team as a group of experts with strong personalities and opinions. In the past, they had tried taking personality assessments to promote better communication, but the dynamic hadn't really changed, and they were back to square one.

I began by asking Fred for an example of the sniping he had

witnessed. He described the way one key player criticized a colleague's meeting facilitation and complained that it was non-productive. That had led to a chilly distance between the two colleagues.

The example wasn't much to go on, but it gave me a hunch. These two—and perhaps others on the team—probably lacked a coherent process for solving problems *together*. They could also have conflicting preferences for different parts of the problem-solving process and different expectations of what should happen in their meetings.

To test my hypothesis, I turned to Basadur Applied Innovation and its system for creative problem-solving to briefly describe four styles of entrepreneurship which directly relate to problem-solving stages.

Four Styles of Leadership

People have natural preferences or styles for approaching the different stages of problem-solving. Basadur refers to them as *Generators, Conceptualizers, Optimizers,* and *Implementers.* These leadership styles represent the problem-solving stages of *Generating, Conceptualizing, Optimizing,* and *Implementing* respectively. Each leadership style— and stage—is important for achieving results. When team members don't understand how they fit together, predictable tensions can arise.

1. Generators: Identify Problems and Opportunities

As problem-solving cycles begin, some individuals naturally identify new problems and opportunities in their customer space. Although it may seem to happen serendipitously, the truth is, these people have strong connection-making skills. Generators seem to have a gift for making connecting ideas that others don't. They instinctively draw from conversations, observations, or direct experiences that take place inside or outside the organization. They often seem to have an endless supply of new possibilities and enjoy getting things started. They are

Four Styles of Entrepreneurial Leadership

DIRECT EXPERIENCE

Implementer

Getting it done in the real world, action, results

- Know enough to get going
- Adapt to changing circumstances
- Enthusiastic but impatient
- Bring others on board, but dislike apathy

Generator

Getting things started

- New problems, challenges, possibilities
- Value different perspectives
- Create options (diverge) rather than evaluate
  - Enjoy ambiguity
  - Keep options open

EVALUATION

IDEATION

Turning ideas into practical solutions and plans

- Analytical thinking
- Appreciate well defined problems
- Find the critical few factors
- Evaluate options rather than diverge
- See little value in "dreaming"
- Dislike ambiguity

Defining problems, understanding big picture connections

- Putting ideas together & new insights
- Abstract thinking
- Clear understanding necessary
- High sensitivity to and appreciation of ideas
- Not concerned with moving to action

Optimizer

Conceptualizer

ABSTRACT THINKING

Graphic adapted and used with permission of Marino (Min) Basadur, the developer of the Simplexity Thinking System for improving workplace innovation and creativity.

interested in WHAT. *What's going on? What's new? What problem can be solved? What opportunity might be grasped?*

2. Conceptualizers: Understand and Define Problems

The second phase of problem-solving requires people who like to connect the dots among data points. They convert their findings into potential solutions to the problem or opportunity. Conceptualizers use abstract reasoning to pull the information together and come up with some initial concepts for a solution. They are frequently adept at strategy. They are interested in WHY. *Why is this problem important? They want to see the big picture. Also, they want to understand the problem and discover the most impactful way to define it as an opportunity.*

3. Optimizers: Develop Practical Solutions

As potential solutions evolve from a Conceptualizer's efforts, we require people who can sort through those solutions by developing realistic criteria for evaluating them. Optimizers determine which solutions practically meet client needs and, with consideration of internal company resources, they formulate plans to implement those solutions.

Optimizers execute in a disciplined manner to move a product to market. Using abstract, critical reasoning, they evaluate the pros and cons of different solutions. They are most likely to be interested in HOW. *How do we develop a plan to bring the ideas to reality? How do we decide who will take the lead for different parts of the plan?*

4. Implementers: Putting Innovations and Solutions to Work

The cycle of problem-solving is completed only when an organization's solution is accepted by its customers. Now it's up to Implementers to compile the efforts of Generators, Conceptualizers, and Optimizers and confirm the validity of their efforts. Implementers like selling solutions. They're very good at evaluating the people and resources necessary to get things done. They are flexible, adapting on the spot when a situation turns out to be different than originally planned or anticipated. For them, primary interest lies in WHERE and WHEN. *Where and when can we get started? Where and when do we need to get acceptance of this before we can go ahead?*

After sharing these entrepreneurial styles and the stages of problem-solving they represent with Fred, I sensed relief and an "aha moment" in our discussion. His team might not be dealing with deeply rooted personality issues but rather how each of them could better fit into a coherent process.

Identifying Thinking Styles: The Basadur Profile

Once Fred understood the leadership styles, I led him through the eight steps of the Basadur Simplexity process. The process incorporates the four stages and leadership styles we just examined. Each step is critical to achieving the desired outcome.

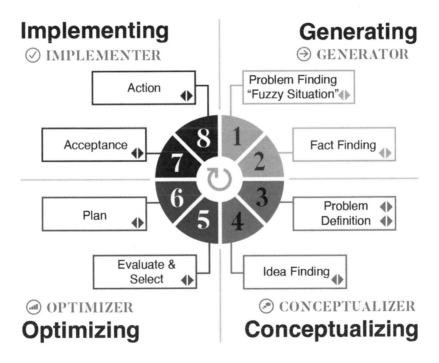

The Entrepreneurial Cycle

Graphic adapted and used with permission of Marino (Min) Basadur, the developer of the Simplexity Thinking System for improving workplace innovation and creativity.

After my brief description, Fred recognized the relationship between the stages of problem-solving and the steps required to achieve an innovative result. He noted that none of his team were particularly adept at planning (Step 6 in the process pictured, undertaken by Optimizers).

Although Fred had mentally attributed a leadership style to each of his team members, he was intrigued to find out if his hunches were correct. All team members agreed to take the brief Basadur Innovation Profile that measures the preferences people naturally have for different stages of the process.

Team plotting revealed that Fred was right: no one had Optimizer as a primary preference. They simply tried implementing the different solutions they came up with to see which ones gained traction. That rapid prototyping approach led to some successes, but it also prevented the team from developing solutions with enough features to meet client needs. One person on the team with Optimizer as a secondary preference could flex to that role but knew she wouldn't be able to manage it for long. Ideally, the company would add someone exhibiting a natural Optimizer preference to the team.

In our team debrief, the leaders identified their individual styles, where they most added value, and under what situations they might take their inclinations too far. Reflecting on previous experiences, they were able to recognize the value each leadership style brought to the team.

We discussed common conflicts that frequently arise between Generating and Optimizing—many ideas versus one good or practical one—as well as the inherent tensions between Conceptualizing and Implementation—thinking things through versus acting right away. The team expressed a sense of relief, the laughter of recognition, and even fascination at this new lens on their interactions. Now they wanted to move forward and learn how to practically use the process in their own meetings.

Testing the Basadur Profile Results with Problem-Solving

A few weeks later, we met again to take Fred's team through the entire Basadur Simplexity process and test an approach for conducting creative, problem-solving meetings.

Through each of the steps, the facilitator wrote team members' ideas on paper. Then the team evaluated which were the best or most important ones. This organized process *diverged* on many ideas while deferring judgment and then *converged* them into a critical few ideas. The process brought out team members' differing perspectives and creativity, and they expressed appreciation for how the logical flow of the stages helped them identify the real problem they needed to solve. By the end, they had arrived at some solutions with a sense of confidence in their thought process and a feeling of closer connection to each other.

Several months later, Fred described their transition this way. "The biggest takeaway seems to be an awareness of whether we're converging or diverging. That awareness allows the conversation to flow differently. We used to pick our priorities and leap to execution. Now we have priorities, but we recognize that these priorities probably aren't fully crystallized. In the first few weeks or so, we have more tolerance to tighten the process earlier, before we start implementing. So, we are starting to see the importance of all the steps required to achieve success."[1]

Leadership Thinking Styles

After consulting with CEOs and executive leaders, I've seen how greatly an individual's style preference can impact their own and their company's success. Whatever leaders intentionally value—and their blind spots—create invisible boundaries for employees. Employees

---

1   This and other interview remarks have been edited for length and clarity.

will adapt to the way leaders talk and what they emphasize. Leaders can subtly adapt to fill in for the team's blind spots too.

I interviewed other senior practitioners of the Basadur Simplexity process for their perceptions of its impact. Together, we had accumulated about 100 years of working with teams and their leaders. While there were expected overlaps in our experiences, each practitioner pointed out uniquely valuable reflections and insights.[2]

The way leaders' predominant styles impact organizations are not consistent across all contexts. In reality, anyone can shift styles, depending on what the situation requires, and the cognitive work demands at that time. These are states of thinking and action rather than fixed personality traits, but they each play important roles in the entrepreneurial cycle.

The Generator Leader

Generator leaders are the ones in shortest supply in most organizations. Globally, only about 17% of company professionals are Generators.[3]

As senior leaders, Generators are often risk-takers. They may be brought into risky situations where great success and failure are both possible. When successful, their leadership can create an innovation culture and make their company an entrepreneurial factory. This style of leadership is the closest to the true entrepreneur inside an organization.

Here's how one Generator leader described his approach as head of a hospital marketing department: "I find that ideas come from

---

2   For a deeper exploration of reflections and insights on the Basadur Simplexity process, see the following article: Andy Wu, Goran Calic, and Min Basadur, "4 Types of Innovators Every Organization Needs," *Harvard Business Review,* October 27, 2022, https://hbr.org/2022/10/4-types-of-innovators-every-organization-needs.

3   Dr. Min Basadur, "Basadur Applied Creativity Skill-Building Workshops," (workbook), ©1981, 1996, 2002, 2012.

listening very closely to people and taking little snippets from what they say. I listen for ideas that will take me down a beneficial path. It could also be a flop, and I would be okay with that. By nature, I take more risks. In healthcare there aren't many Generators because they must manage risk."

Later, this leader became the president of the first hospital of its kind in his state. He had many ideas about how to break new ground in healthcare. However, his vision came with many challenges. "We were pushing the limit on too many things. You can't innovate in all areas all the time. You have to give people a break. There needs to be a cadence. You have to be sensitive to how much innovation the organization can take at one time."

Like many Generators, he was high on optimism. "Even if things are falling apart, I can find the silver lining. The downside is knowing that people are wondering, 'Does he have a clue? Does he really understand how challenging this is?'"

To use a baseball analogy, Generators swing for the fences. They may not reach the fence, but they'll get closer than might otherwise be possible.

The Conceptualizer Leader

Slightly more than 19% of professionals are Conceptualizers.[4]

One business unit leader in the construction industry is very successful in selling to senior-level clients. He asks many questions to understand what they are trying to accomplish. Mentally, he connects the dots and then offers one or two solutions for how the structure might be built to address the client's needs. He then translates the overall concept to the Optimizers and Implementers at different levels in his company—using practical language they understand—so they can move forward into estimates and plans.

His tailored approach to business development has won trust and

---

4   Ibid.

much repeat business.

Another talented Conceptualizer was intentionally recruited by the board because the company—led by a strong Implementer—was falling behind its competitors. When board members were educated about the different leadership styles, they believed they needed a Conceptualizer as CEO to figure out new products and new markets. When a Conceptualizer came on board as president, he was often strategically years ahead of his leadership team, who were largely Optimizers and Implementers. He had many ideas about how to achieve his strategies—so many in fact, that it was a real challenge for him to rein in the number of solutions occurring to him.

He successfully used coaching to find more effective ways of getting people on board. "It took a whole lot of work to gain their buy-in on the right concepts. That was challenging up front. I spent a good six months to a year having meetings across different departments to make them feel like some of those concepts were theirs. Getting the buy-in to the concepts took a lot more deliberate effort, but once we got there, the rest was a whole lot more fun."

Sometimes a senior leader can stay stuck in Conceptualization. One of my interview subjects, who teaches the Simplexity problem-solving process in a large global corporation, had this to say: "In one team we had a number of leaders who were Conceptualizers. They would conceive of a solution and try to run with the idea without having criteria. They weren't passing through the right strategy to activate. They weren't being robust. This risks running in eight different directions with conceptual ideas for solutions. Without narrowing those ideas down to a critical few, they weren't getting to a concrete activation plan."

Going back to our baseball analogy Conceptualizers might ask, "Is this the right game for us to be playing?

Generators and Conceptualizers may determine that they have done the most valuable work of the problem-solving process by coming up with broad ideas and concepts for solutions, thus making what to do next relatively obvious. However, their contributions may go nowhere if they don't move through the next stages and translate them into practical reality. This is when optimizers shine.

The Optimizer Leader

Optimizers—about 28% of professionals—are good at evaluating what is in place and deciding whether it is operating as effectively and efficiently as needed.[5] Sometimes they will take a model that worked in one market or context and adapt it to a new situation with similar dynamics. Very often, professional service firms in engineering, law, or finance are started by Optimizers. They may sense that they have a superior way of doing things and dream of having a business based on high-quality offerings.

Optimizers are very strong on convergence. They want you to communicate to them the few most critical factors to know. They are also strong on process and action planning. A common focus is how to quickly deliver the results for an action plan.

One large law firm stood up an "innovation team." Its essential work was to help the firm's lawyers adopt newer technologies. Their internal customers wanted to improve the efficiency of their own work and sometimes offer the same solutions to client companies.

The Generators and Conceptualizers on the team were frustrated because researching new ideas for improved technologies was discouraged. Suggesting different ways of framing the problem was generally a non-starter.

Considering much of legal thinking is based on precedent, this is not surprising. If Generators like to "swing for the fences," Optimizers go for "solid singles and doubles," believing that more can be achieved through small, incremental improvements.

The Implementer Leader

---

5   Ibid.

The Implementer style is the most commonly occurring one. A full 41% of people in the Basadur global database of over 100,000 profiles prefer Implementation.[6] Early career employees often begin as Implementers while they learn what they are expected to practically accomplish in their roles. They may change styles with different work demands.

Some company leaders rise through the ranks while retaining the Implementer style; that approach gained them a reputation for getting things done. Indeed, these are the people who can be counted on to deliver results. Their creative adaptability allows them to meet the circumstances of the moment. They have a strong bias for action and can be impatient with others whom they might perceive as "over-thinkers."

Implementers are by far the most common leaders appearing in manufacturing and construction companies. For them, bringing projects in on time, at cost, and on schedule make the difference between profitability or loss.

Most leaders simply want to make their numbers, so they're cautious about taking risks and rocking the boat. In some cases, they don't even want people to point out problems that can be fixed. They may even laugh at a leader whose idea didn't work. At senior levels, it's hard for Implementers to take risks when no one else is on board.

Some Implementers, who have come up through the ranks with a reputation for "getting things done," can quickly assume that if things are not going well, they need to take over. They continue to behave as they had earlier in their careers rather than completing the entrepreneurial cycle by delegating work to leaders of different styles. In baseball terms, they focus on situational awareness. They're ready for whatever comes up, and they adapt quickly.

Leaders in the Center

Some leaders do not have a strong preference for any one stage of

---

6   Ibid.

the cycle. This is not uncommon among entrepreneurs, who are initially responsible for all aspects of their product, from idea to delivery. The closer they are to the center, the easier it is for them to understand all of the styles. They'll have the ability to modulate their own behavior, not get stuck too long in any stage, and eventually delegate tasks to others and free themselves up to focus on building the business and interacting with customers.

This turned out to be the style of Fred, the CEO in the opening story. Because he understood the stages of the entrepreneurial cycle, Fred could clearly see the value of each one and delegate its oversight to another leader.

"My job as a CEO is to get the pieces in place so that if I'm hit by a bus, it's going to be there for the long term," he told me.

Team Building for Business Results

Insightful leaders know how to bring different functions in their organizations together to solve enterprise problems. In one example, a household goods manufacturing company asked for help with their product development team. The vice presidents (VPs) from each function attended the meetings, but an increasing gridlock slowed down the process.

Instead of collaborating as they needed to, each function was more concerned about protecting their own agenda. There was plenty of finger-pointing over which group was responsible for the delays.

Because the team of VPs was Implementer-heavy, there had been no impetus to change their patterns. The team leader, whom we'll call Ted, happened to be evenly split between Generator and Implementer. He was very frustrated and asked me for help.

At first, Ted envisioned some sort of team-building exercise to build better relationships. I recommended building the team while also solving an important business problem together. Ted was clear that his team of VPs would be more open to a business focus than one that seemed human resources or "feeling oriented."

We scheduled an all-day meeting offsite. Each VP was interviewed to discover their individual perception of what needed to change. Then we presented the issues the VPs had described to the group. We showed them their group profile and led a discussion about their team dynamic to help them understand the entrepreneurial cycle, and we guided them through the thinking style of each of the four preferences.

As we worked through the process, their engagement grew. The process was psychologically safe because everyone was asked to candidly lay out their thoughts. "Crazy" ideas during each divergence phase were encouraged and celebrated. The process flow structure didn't allow more dominant or opinionated members to take over. By the end, they came up with many practical solutions and jointly owned the plan to solve them. Beers and snacks ended the day on a high note. Barriers had come down, and the VPs were clearly better connected to each other than at the start.

By the next year when Ted invited us back, the new product development process was working much better. This time, they had a more strategic approach to problem-solving. They brought in the CEO to help them make changes. Proud of their new culture of collaboration, they proactively brought in customers as team members too. Customer involvement turned the process into a co-creation exercise that shortened and enhanced the product development cycle, increasing the probability that they would secure their customer's business.

Facilitating Cross-Cultural Entrepreneurship

A woman I'll call Inge, another Generator-Implementer leader, was on a holding company leadership team in Europe. She was trained in the Simplexity Method and clearly recognized that, with equal preferences, her tendency was to generate multiple ideas while hoping to execute on all of them.

"If I try to solve the problem and it doesn't work, I'm probably trying to solve the wrong problem. Then I need to go back to problem definition," she told me.

To avoid the downsides of her preferences, she maintains a peer mentoring relationship with another woman—let's call her Elise—a senior leader in another country and company. Elise is strong in Conceptualization and Optimization. Since both of them are trained to facilitate the Simplexity entrepreneurial process, they recognize the value of their complementary thinking styles to help each other work through challenges.

Inge and Elise also recognize the styles of other work colleagues. They deliberately leverage them to bring together diverse thinking and skill sets that create vibrant work environments and greater value in an ongoing way.

Interestingly, both women described taking the role of facilitator and leader in planning and problem-solving meetings. They find this particularly helpful in working with other colleagues from at least 16 country backgrounds. They give everyone an equal voice to raise issues and develop solutions acceptable to everyone.

Effective Entrepreneurial Leaders Know How to Sell

Most times, the success or failure of entrepreneurial leaders is based in their ability to work with the different styles of those inside their organization who can affect their ability to make change. More than one promising change initiative by a Generator or Conceptualizer has been scuttled by a board of directors who leaned strongly toward Implementation. Key members either didn't understand why the company should embark on something different or were simply risk-averse.

Great entrepreneurial leaders need to be very good at Step 7 of the problem-solving process: *Gaining Acceptance*. That's what they spend a lot of their time doing. People don't really resist *change*, they resist *being* changed. At some level, most people need to feel a sense of ownership in any change that's going to affect them or others who matter to them.

A stakeholder analysis becomes invaluable: *who are the people or groups in the company who can get you either celebrated or fired?* Consider their likely problem-solving style and what's important to them. For some it might be about job security, for others, profitability. How will you frame the message in the context of job security or improved profitability? The selling points for one person can be different than the selling points for others. Some people may consider potential obstacles that suggest the proposed solution might not work. They anticipate obstacles and prepare to respond to them.

As one senior consultant observed, "You need to modulate your behavior constantly to maximize the value you're creating. You might be a Conceptualizer, but you may need to have an Implementation conversation."

One leader reporting to his board noticed that certain members would become interested, annoyed, or questioning, depending on how he framed the conversation. He identified three probable leadership styles in one meeting: Conceptualizer, Optimizer, and Implementer. Afterward, we discussed how his initiative might be framed with the styles and concerns of each leadership style in mind. He noted that a CEO who is recruiting board members may find greater efficiency by considering problem-solving styles along with relevant experience in the final selection. This can help mitigate "group think" in their advice and direction.

This leader also made a point of attending important project meetings led by managers and noted, "I find Optimizers and Implementers are very efficient at running day-to-day meetings. They want to focus on the task and move it forward. If I am not reading the crowd or the room right, I'll get off on a conceptual tangent. That can get me uninvited for future meetings."

A Conceptualizer leader, whose boss was an Optimizer, had to moderate talking about all of his great ideas. For the boss to truly hear him, he had to focus on a few critical points.

Team Selection and Engagement

Managing all four stages of problem-solving is easier when it's cognitively diverse, that is, composed of members representing all four styles of leadership. They can utilize their combined wisdom to creatively solve problems together. More likely they will ensure that a phase is not overlooked, even when they feel pressured to just take action.

Effective leaders consider ways to recruit team members who are cognitively diverse rather than following the common impulse to choose like-minded people. Research shows that heterogenous teams consistently outperform homogenous ones. Their leaders ensure employee engagement by giving people of all preferences room to feel heard and acknowledged as true contributors.

It's vitally important that the activities taking place in all four stages of the entrepreneurship cycle are both attractive and motivating for everyone, regardless of their leadership style.

Summary

In organizations large and small, one of the most important things that an entrepreneurial leader can do is respond to their marketspace by solving the company's biggest opportunities and challenges with a strategic team approach. Leaders and their team members have preferences for how they like to engage in problem-solving with each other.

Generators like getting things started and finding new problems and opportunities.

Conceptualizers like defining problems, understanding the big picture, and putting ideas together.

Optimizers like turning abstract ideas into practical solutions and plans.

Implementers like getting things done in the real-world involving action and results.

Each style has a pivotal role to play in the entrepreneurial cycle of developing the products or services their customers need. A balance of leadership styles creates an efficient flow through all stages of solution management. The senior leader's style can impact what gets acknowledged as important and what is overlooked in any business.

To maintain the engagement of key people, *your* entrepreneurial style matters. Make it your mission to understand how individual members of your team think about and engage with problems. Doing so draws out their best skills. It values and rewards the contributions of everyone on your team and creates powerful results.

Acknowledgments: The author appreciates the support of Min Basadur, the developer of the Simplexity Thinking System. He provided assistance from the early stages of developing this chapter through the final stages of editing. He has graciously given permission to use and adapt the graphics displayed here.

CHAPTER 7

BALANCE AND SYNERGY

Matthew Holland

Socialpreneur, Thought Leader, Vet, and CEO of Synergistic Creations, Inc.

bal·ance /ˈbaləns/: The condition in which different elements are equal or in the correct proportions, creating an even distribution of weight enabling someone or something to remain upright and steady.

syn·er·gy /ˈsinərjē/: The interaction of elements that when combined produce a total effect that is greater than the sum of the individual elements.[7]

So, we're successful, made millions of dollars or maybe billions, created generational wealth, or preserved or grew the wealth handed down to us. But with all of this, what kind of human beings are we? What kind of humanity are we creating with our actions?

No matter what our beliefs are, most of us understand that life and everything in it is an expression of some form of energy. Industry titans understand this. They use the energy patterns in their niches to create greater returns and take the lion's share of their market segment. This

---

7   "Oxford Languages and Google - English." Oxford Languages, Oxford Languages, 2022, https://languages.oup.com/google-dictionary-en/.

is no different than a farmer who understands the right crops to plant, the right time to plant those crops, the right soil to plant them in, and the right amount of water, light, and nutrients to add. Together, these factors create a synergy that allows him to reap the greatest reward from what he sowed.

The right energy inputs produce the greatest positive outcome, but the opposite is also true. Utilizing energy in the wrong way creates negative results. This has been going on for too long: the more money or influence someone has, the more power they have to shape reality. The world has endured more than enough wealthy people who have no desire to give back to the societies who created their wealth, no desire to help change humanity for the better.

What we say, what we do, the choices we make, and the paths we take, impact others with an expanding ripple effect. Actions move from one person to the next, creating either balance with positive energy or imbalance with negative energy. That impact expands to families, workplaces, communities, social networks, and even countries. The ripples echo on and on in ways both seen and unseen.

As human beings first, and established business leaders and entre-preneurs second, we can choose the type of energy we put into the world and whether we create balance or imbalance. It's just that simple.

Balance and Synergy in Action

The easiest way to explain balance and synergy in action is not through humans but rather through birds, specifically starling murmu-rations. Stop for a moment, grab your nearest intern-enabled device, and watch the first 30 seconds of *National Geographic*'s video, *Starlings Fly in Mesmerizing Shape-Shifting Cloud Formation.*[8] Through highly coordinated swoops, turns, and dives, these birds demonstrate synergy

---

8   *Starlings Fly in Mesmerizing Shape-Shifting Cloud Formation,* National Geo-graphic, December 16, 2016, video, https://www.nationalgeographic.com/animals/article/starling-murmuration-swarm-video.

in action. Most stunning to mere mortals, these birds react with such synchronization and so quickly; if not immediately, within a couple of wing flaps. They move almost as one.

I was mesmerized by my first "live" experience of watching a murmuration of starlings constantly fold and stretch, overlap, and compress. The hair on my arms stood straight up. Moving in synchronicity, even when separated from the larger body, they were constantly drawn back together, and they reminded me of the rhythmically flowing waves that gently touch and recede from our collective country's shores.

These murmurations are self-organized, meaning they have no single leader. Their synchronized behavior allows them to continuously change direction almost simultaneously. It's "the rapid transmission of local behavioral response to neighbors" that enables such startling synchronicity, according to journalist John Donovan.[9] Their balanced synergy results from bottom-up and not top-down control. Donovan states this is only possible because each bird keeps tabs on its seven closest neighbors and ignores all else. These little groups of seven touch on other individuals and other groups of seven, twisting and turning, until the whole murmuration moves together. These little winged creatures stay in the flow of balance and synergy because they singularly and collectively react to any forces that might create imbalance.

Negative Energy

During my time in the United States Air Force boot camp, the Military Training Instructor (MTI) assigned to my barracks entered at O-Dark-Early after having a huge argument with his partner. He charged through the barracks like a raging inferno, tossing over bunk beds, emptying footlockers, and throwing the contents across the room at any trainee within range, and particularly, at our Dorm Chief. The

---

9   John Donovan, "The Secrets and Science Behind Starling Murmurations," August 9, 2019. HowStuffWorks.com, August 9, 2019, https://animals.howstuffworks.com/birds/starling-murmurations.htm.

MTI screamed obscenities while raging about the argument he'd had, very colorfully telling us how completely inept we all were.

The Dorm Chief sustained the worst of the MTI's rage, and the rest of us suffered because of it. We spent nearly 16 hours that day cleaning and recleaning the barracks while the Dorm Chief screamed at us in the same way our MTI had screamed at him. Anyone who dared speak out found themselves with their backs against the wall, sitting midair, legs shaking in their imaginary chairs.

We were only allowed one meal that day: dinner. While everyone else stood in line ahead of us, rank and file, our Dorm Chief had another punishment in mind. For 30 minutes, we held a low plank position, suspended 6 – 12 inches horizontally above the concrete using only our forearms and toes. After what seemed like eons, we were able to enter the chow hall, but we had only a few minutes left to eat, and many of us barely had the strength to raise the food from our trays.

For the remainder of that week, every trainee seethed with anger, animosity, and hatred. Negativity continually rippled back and forth between us. Meanwhile, the MTI who created the initial surge of angry energy was nowhere to be seen.

Currently, the world seems tangled in ever-increasing imbalance. The pendulum continues to slam to the far extremes of left and right, always missing the balance of center. The state of our collective environments, both internally and externally, is continually in and out of flux. We are unstable and unbalanced. Imbalance heightens a growing sense of fear and doom. Unfortunately, some people and entities manipulate that fear and doom to exert power and control, which triggers a sustained state of fight-or-flight. Stress, anxiety, depression, anger, rage, and hatred result.

We can find this imbalance in every corner of the world. Just look at the headlines across any news media. The vast majority of them are designed to trigger fear and anxiety. The White House refuses to release this. The Left is trying to do that. The Right is attempting to do something else. Deaths in 2022 were among the worst in 50 years because of COVID-19—or the vaccine—depending upon your perspective. The same polarization can be seen in advertising, marketing, and the manner in which new proposed laws or hot button issues are heralded to the masses.

So why does this matter?

It matters because everything is, at some level, interconnected with everything else, and if we're not careful, things break. Most often, when power and money run amuck, our sense of connection and community breaks, and so does our awareness of how much we need these things. Decades of putting profit before the people who consume the product or service and those who make or create them can no longer be tolerated. Attitudes are changing direction. We're all looking for answers.

Science Has the Answers

I recently bought a shirt from Uniqlo with a quote from Shinya Yamanaka, who won a Nobel Prize for identifying cells that can be reprogrammed to become other types of cells. Above the image of a human double helix genome, the T-shirt states: "Technologies progress. Humanity must progress." Below the image, it says: "Science progresses. Humanity must progress." As time moves forward, so should we, in the manner with which we approach life.

You see, beneath the surface of every action and interaction, science is at work. All of life—its processes, the way we see it, and everything we know about it—follows specific, balanced, and purposeful patterns. At the quantum level, everything is comprised of atoms, which are made up of protons, neutrons, and electrons, each balanced in their own unique ways. Together and balanced, they create many forms of synergy.

We can also think of synergy as the age-old summertime potato sack race. The winners are typically the two individuals who together work as a team, moving in sync with each other, balancing out each other's strengths and limitations. They establish a flow that achieves maximum speed and takes them across the finish line first. Those who don't reach synergy typically stumble and fall behind them.

Without balance and synergy, nothing survives. Think about failed civilizations. Most often they lacked the ability to stay in the balance, in the flow and thus either fell out of/or short of the synergy we are all looking to achieve. Eventually reaching instead a place of discord, resulting in accelerating entropy, and the chaos within those imbalances escalating them toward a looming extinction of what they were and had been.

Creating balance and synergy doesn't mean that everything is all sunshine, roses, and just ducky. It doesn't mean everyone is all kumbaya with one another and in full agreement about everything. Instead, it results in an ability to be fully present and mindful, moving forward with a positive and balanced direction, regardless of what is occurring externally. Ultimately, being able to stay in sync, in balance, and in the flow of synergy while taking in and adapting to or pushing away forces that strive to create imbalances.

"All negativity is caused by an accumulation of psychological time and denial of the present. Unease, anxiety, tension, stress, worry—all forms of fear—are caused by too much future, and not enough presence. Guilt, regret, resentment, grievances, sadness, bitterness, and all forms of non-forgiveness are caused by too much past, and not enough presence."[10]

Okay, wow. I'll admit, that is a lot to digest, and honestly, how or what exactly does that have to do with being a successful entrepreneur or leader? Too much past and not enough presence has a lot to do with just about everything. Without internal and external balance, we create forms of conflict that alter the reality of self and everything around us, including our endeavors, often in unintended and counterproductive ways.

---

10   Eckart Tolle, *The Power of Now: A Guide to Spiritual Enlightenment*. (Novato, CA: New World Library, 2004).

I know; that may sound like a whole lot of yaw, yaw, blah, blah, blah, but—trust me—there is rhyme to this reasoning and a rationale to realize. It all comes down to leading by example in everything we do and everything we say while being mindful about how we affect others.

It's time to look beyond how much money we can rake in. There are five concrete ways to do that.

1. Recognize Patterns

Everything in the known universe has a pattern, a very succinct and finite recipe, that allows balance and synergy to occur. Or not. From the molecular structure that makes a rock a rock to the balanced chaos that allows a star to exist, everything results from patterns of energy.

Stop and think about how often news media reports on individuals or companies that are imbalanced by internal or external stressors and ultimately fall from grace. As they fall like dominoes, other entities around them also begin to stagger, fall, or implode.

To usher in the return of balance and synergy, we each must do our part internally and externally. A fully balanced "me" creates a balanced "we." As we find balance, it creates positive changes in others around us. Those changes help them find balance, and then—you guessed it—that positive energy pattern continues to expand in ever-widening circles.

2. Recognize Knowledge Limitations

In addition, it's important to realize that you, me—we—know virtually nothing in the grand scheme of things. It doesn't matter if we are Nobel Prize Laureates, MENSA members, heads of nations, Fortune 500 Executives, or plumbers; we only know what falls within our limited areas of experience. When we believe we know everything, we're doomed. We've locked ourselves off from the vast wisdom available through the people we encounter, the internet, and various forms of media everywhere around us.

As entrepreneurs, we've all had epiphanies, those quintessential "aha moments" when some force awakened us to broaden our perspective and understanding. The ideas and values we bring to our roles are a mix of nature and nurture downloaded from the latitudes and longitudes in which we developed, the soil in which our gardens of knowledge grew.

Like the farmer who knows how to adjust the soil to grow the best crops, we must adjust our soil—our perspectives—to grow. When we think we have the answers to everything, we have the answers for nothing. We may know but don't truly see.

3. Practice Dimensional Thinking and Being

As successful leaders, entrepreneurs, public figures, and anyone else who falls into the "influencer" fold, we need to practice three-dimensional thinking (3D) in tandem with a fifth-dimensional state of being (5D).

Matthew Kutz is credited with coining the phrase "3D thinking." He defines it this way:

Thinking in 3D requires asking and answering questions that pertain to the past, present, and future all at the same time. An uncertain world requires people to instantly and intuitively adapt . . . integrating knowledge of past events with the acute awareness of the present and the preferred future.[11]

After reading numerous research papers and sifting through many books regarding states of consciousness, I found Erin Sharaf's explanation of a 5D state of being the best:

The fifth dimension is not a place; it's a level of consciousness which is higher than the one we've been living in. . . . In the fifth dimension, people are not motivated by greed and fear as we are now, but by a sense of respect and love for all beings of the earth. . . . They know that all of life is sacred, and that there is enough of what we need to go

---

11   Matthew Kutz, *Contextual Intelligence* (London: Palgrave Macmillan, 2017), pg. 99 – 107, https://doi.org/10.1007/978-3-319-44998-2_8.

around—if we start making wise and compassionate choices. There is no mental baggage or false sense of duality. The illusion of separation is gone. In the fifth dimension, people live primarily from the heart and not the mind, which is a much more powerful way to manifest.[12]

These concepts combine to create a roadmap for moving forward. Understanding that what we say and do matters, we must recognize our thoughts—past, present, and future—before we form them into words and actions. We can either act with awareness and responsibility, changing the future for the better, or we can take actions that damn us all to H-E-L-L.

Being open and aware demonstrates that we are all in this together, just as we always have been and always will be. By choosing selflessness over selfishness and inclusion over exclusion, we have opportunities to positively influence the world. By teaching others how to fish rather than trying to sell them fish or manipulate them into buying fish, we can make a positive long-term impact. By being individuals with depth of being, which we pass on, instead of allowing others listening to drown in the shallow waters of our words, we show ourselves to be true leaders.

4. Lead With Compassion and Empathy

Seek altruism, lead with compassion, and guide others with empathy. I had the honor of hearing the founder and director of the Center for Compassion and Altruism Research and Education, James R. Doty, speak about those qualities. He has also written about them, drawing upon his experience as a neurologist and neurosurgeon.

"While science has made great strides in treating pathologies of the human mind, far less research exists to date on positive qualities of the human mind including compassion, altruism, and empathy. Yet, these prosocial traits are innate to us and lie at the very centerpiece of

---

12   Erin Sharaf, "We're Entering into the 5th Dimension of Consciousness," *Elephant Journal*, January 20, 2018, https://www.elephantjournal.com/2018/01/yr-were-entering-into-the-5th-dimension-of-consciousness/.

our common humanity. Our capacity to feel compassion has ensured the survival and thriving of our species over millennia."[13]

It is time to nurture these qualities and help others thrive, and hold ourselves accountable for our actions, leading by that example.

5. Strive for Balanced Exchanges

We should strive to achieve balance or fairness in all of our exchanges. Exchanges really just break down into four categories:

A black hole exchange occurs when one party takes all or gives all. It creates a vacuum and a negative balance. Think of this like a house that is a money pit or car that is a lemon. Each and every time you throw money at the problem, something else breaks.

A minimal exchange, another example of imbalance, takes place when very little is given for what is received. I like to think of this like a Scooby Snack; it's just a morsel and never enough for the deed that Scooby or Shaggy completes.

A balanced exchange unfolds when the flow of give-and-take is balanced. It ultimately leads to synergy. This is where you want to be. It's like the winning team in the potato sack race in a nutshell; teammates share an even give-and-take, creating a balance that ultimately leads to synergy. Synergy wins the race.

An abundant exchange happens when we step up and lean in, providing abundance to those who are in need or as an expression of gratitude.

When we remove imbalance from our relational, physical, mental, emotional, business, personal, monetary, and all other exchanges, we create a balance that overflows to all aspects of life. Balance gives synergy free access.

Take notice of all your daily exchanges. Are they balanced? For any that are not, redirect your approach by selecting an action from the

---

13   James R. Doty, "The Center for Compassion and Altruism Research and Education (CCARE)," The Center for Compassion and Altruism Research and Education, Stanford University, 2005, http://ccare.stanford.edu/.

following list of directional choices:

Promote all of the balanced exchanges to your closest inner circles.

Demote minimal exchange or proceed to directional choice #3.

Vote any black hole exchanges completely off your island. Don't engage in them! Avoid any behavior that invites them into your life.

Once you are able to balance your exchanges, you'll bring continual balance into your life, which will then radiate into others' lives. Be aware that this is a continual process. Even a single black hole or minimal exchange risks inviting chaos, discord, and entropy back into the equation.

Most importantly, once you have perfected this process, teach it to others.

In a Nutshell

When we lead by example with mindfulness, compassion, empathy, and balance, our behavior resonates within the consciousness of our circles of influence. This, in turn, creates change in their behavior, which radiates within their circles of influence. This domino effect results in an explosion of symmetry. Remember:

Everything has a pattern, and those patterns create balance or imbalance. Strive to create balance.

Keep your mind open to all forms of knowledge, ideas, and points of view. If you don't, you've donned blinders to the wisdom around you.

Understand that we learn from the past; we don't live in it. Be present, balanced, and zentered (zenfully centered) in your own here and now. Use the first two steps in this list to plan for your preferred future but know others will exist there too, and to manifest it accordingly.

Be selfless, show compassion and empathy, and embrace altruism because we are all in this together just as we always have been and always will be.

Finally, create balanced equations across your entire life, remove the imbalances, and pay it forward by teaching others to do the same.

It is our responsibility as successful leaders, entrepreneurs, influencers, and public figures to help usher in an era of balance and synergy. Abundance is possible for everyone. We must decide collectively to make it happen. Now is the time.

CHAPTER 8

Leadership & Tax Strategies for Achieving
GENERATIONAL WEALTH

Michael Markiewicz

CPA, Entrepreneur, International Best-Selling Author
Executive Film Producer, Investor, Philanthropist

When most people think about generational wealth, they think in terms of creating enough money to support future generations. That's part of it. However, a great accumulation of wealth brings the potential for much more—like supporting causes that create positive change in the world and even initiating such ventures.

A great objective requires a great strategy, and great strategies begin with the basics: structuring your business to grow and infusing your business with passion. Much has been written about having passion in your vocation. What does that mean for certified public accountants (CPAs) like me who deal with a lot of numbers and spreadsheets for businesses? How can one be passionate about what many perceive to be a rather dry subject?

My answer is that it's not about the numbers, spreadsheets, and accounting and tax systems I utilize in my work. Rather, it's about the results that come about from leading your employees effectively and properly strategizing ways for clients to save money on their tax bills while enhancing their overall financial well-being and possibilities for achieving generational wealth.

Clients who are happy with the results give me the passion to continue doing what I do. It's about having a positive impact on people's lives, and it's about values.

As Tim Cook, CEO of Apple, told graduates at Gallaudet University in 2022, "Lead with your values."[14] He described it as the way to find meaning and fulfillment.

You see, leadership and values are inseparable.

Over the years, I've employed numerous strategies to enhance my clients' financial well-being. I am confident that the following eight strategies can help you achieve generational wealth.

1. Leading Your People

Everything begins with people. Most successful businesses depend on the people who work in that business. This, of course, applies not only to the owner or founder of the business, but the employees or partners who make things happen. Everything else you do is impacted by the way you relate to others.

Never underestimate the power and value of your people.

Development is a key component of ensuring their effectiveness. Your people want to be valued and appreciated. So, what tools are you, as an entrepreneur, giving to them? I take several approaches.

Training

It is imperative to train your people in the skills and technology required to proficiently serve the customers or clients of your organization. Training is ongoing. It's not a one-time deal.

In my practice, the tax and accounting rules change constantly.

---

14   "Apple CEO Tim Cook at Gallaudet University," YouTube, CNET Highlights, Gallaudet University, May 13, 2022, video, 6:13, https://www.youtube.com/watch?v=Kov3mlrYxOM.

Keeping up-to-date with these rules is critical for CPAs. It is equally critical for the staff who handle day-to-day operations. Train your staff to be the next *you*, and your business will still run effectively, even when you aren't there.

Compensation

Pay your people fairly. The assessment of what is "fair" may depend on your geographical location. Consider the standard of living requirements for your region. And consider offering bonuses for exemplary work and for those who go above and beyond the minimal requirements to do a great job.

Give people more than they can handle.

I have a rule with respect to my employee colleagues: give them 100% of the responsibility, and if they meet you at 75% or 80%, you have done a great job of supporting them.

Give people every opportunity for growth. In my experience, when people are given an opportunity for growth—and possibly to step out of their comfort zone—those who are inclined to do so, will.

Encourage Entrepreneurship

Training is a great way to encourage people to be entrepreneurs. Teach the benefits of being "your own boss." Teach them the relationship between risk and reward. Having worked for major and mid-sized accounting firms, I belatedly realized that the grass is never greener working for someone else. I cannot begin to recount how many times I switched jobs hoping to improve my lot, only to discover that the grass was just as brown everywhere else. Fortunately, I came to my senses before it was too late.

I happen to love sustainable lawns that are continually regenerating with succulents and other renewable plants. In my humble opinion, this is the only way to create ongoing generational wealth and happiness in our goals for our professional and personal lives.

Be Charitable

Help others who want to do what you do. Beyond that, be passionate about causes that matter to you. I encourage you to give what you can, how you can, and what you can. The gratification of doing so will exceed your wildest expectations.

Be Generous with Your Time

Most of all, mentor people, encourage them, and don't be afraid that they will replace you. After all, isn't that the goal? I believe in that. I hope you do too. Keep these ideas in mind as you start your business and as it grows.

2. Choice of Business Entity

When establishing a business, determining the correct form of entity can be crucial for maximizing revenue and minimizing expenses. The type of business often dictates the best form of entity. And the jurisdiction where an entity is established is equally important as it could impact the tax burden. The typical forms of entity are *C Corp, S Corp, Partnership, Limited Liability Company (LLC), Sole Proprietorship,* and *Trusts.*

Let's take a closer look at each of them.

C Corps

Most large companies with household names are C Corps, and in many cases, they are organized in Delaware. Why Delaware? It's a very corporate-friendly state with some significant tax advantages. The vast majority of these large companies tend to work with the Big Four accounting firms—Deloitte, Ernst & Young (EY), KPMG, PricewaterhouseCoopers (PwC)—and large well-known law firms. I prefer not to serve this category of clients.

Because my clients don't fall into the C Corp category, I tend to shy away from C Corps. In addition, if a C Corp pays a dividend, there can be double taxation, as the shareholder/owner will be taxed on the dividend, yet the corporation cannot deduct it.

S Corps

Next on the list are S Corporations. These corporations are formed under a particular section of the IRS code. They are considered "pass-through entities," meaning the corporation itself is not subject to tax, but the shareholders and owners are. Depending on which state jurisdiction an S Corporation is formed in, there may very well be state and local taxes at the corporate level.

Partnerships

Partnerships are another form of "pass-through entity." They tend to be less expensive to establish than an S Corp, but they don't offer the corporate veil of liability protection. A partnership would need to be formed by two or more partners, while an S Corp can be formed by one individual.

Limited Liability Companies

Another option is a Limited Liability Company, more commonly referred to as an LLC. Multi-member LLCs are treated like partnerships for tax purposes. In most states, they offer some lability protection. Single-member LLCs are "disregarded" for tax purposes. This means that the entity itself is not subject to tax, but rather the profit and loss is reported on a Schedule C on the owner's personal income tax returns. They are very much like sole proprietorships except that, depending on the state of organization, they offer some limited liability protection. It is imperative that you check with your own state's rules and regulations on this subject. You can contact the Secretary of State's office and your state's Department of Taxation.

Sole Proprietorships

Sole proprietorships can be formed by any individual for any business purpose, in many states, without even having to register them. With this type of entity, there is no liability protection, and the profit or loss is reported on a Schedule C on the individual's tax returns. A sole proprietorship is similar to a single-member LLC, but the LLC may offer some liability protection while the sole proprietorship does not.

Trusts

In a trust, the trustee is the person who holds nominal ownership of the trust property and controls or administers it for the good of one or more beneficiaries.

Trusts take many forms, and because of the various levels of complexity, I will not go into too much detail here. However, note that a "simple trust" is a pass-through entity, and tax is paid at the individual level. A "complex trust" generally pays its own tax.

Trust tax rates tend to be significantly higher than individual rates, so there should be a compelling reason to establish a complex trust. For example, it could be used to determine the disposition of assets during the lifetime of the trust creator and the trust's disposition of assets after the creator's death.

As you can see, determining the type of entity and jurisdiction is very important when setting up a new business.

3. Determining Filing Status

A married couple has options for their filing status; they can file jointly as a couple or separately while single individuals have no choice but to file as an individual.

The head of household status, which offers some tax deductions and can apply to married couples or individuals, has very specific rules about qualification. Those rules have to do with supporting dependents and where those dependents live.

Conventional wisdom for married couples suggests that filing jointly brings the best result in terms of the tax burden. However, this is not always the case—especially for wealthy individuals. For my wealthy clients, I always run different scenarios of filing jointly or separately. One pair of married clients were able to save more than $50,000 by filing separately, which they readily agreed to do.

I have encountered numerous other examples where filing separately yielded a better result than filing jointly. As a CPA, it pays to run the alternative scenarios. It makes for a very happy client.

4. Charitable Vehicles

Other tax strategies for wealthy individuals may include charitable vehicles that maximize the impact of desired charitable giving. I recommend clients establish either a private foundation or a *donor-advised fund* (DAF).

For individuals who would like to have their name on a foundation, it's best to establish a private foundation. Private foundations can be more costly to form and maintain. However, individuals may contribute any amount they choose to the foundation, and they may do so repeatedly to a maximum of 60% of adjusted gross income.

All amounts contributed are eligible for the charitable deduction. Any amounts above the maximum are carried forward and eligible for tax deduction in future years. Each year, the private foundation, whose assets are managed by a bank or financial advisor, distributes funds to charities designated by the creator of the foundation. An IRS formula dictates the minimum amount of such distributions each year.

A DAF is significantly less expensive to establish and maintain than a private foundation but shares some of the same benefits: the donor may contribute any amount they wish, and as often as they wish, and take a charitable deduction subject to the same maximum of 60% of adjusted gross income. Where the private foundation must distribute to charities based on an IRS formula, the DAF is not subject to minimum distributions. As with a private foundation, DAF assets are usually managed by a bank or financial advisor.

A couple of charitable trusts frequently utilized by wealthy individuals are the *charitable lead trust* and the *charitable remainder trust*.

A charitable lead trust distributes income from the invested assets to designated charities. At the end of a specific term or upon death of the trust creator, the remaining assets revert back to the trust's named beneficiaries who can be non-charitable individuals.

A charitable remainder trust is the opposite. This type of trust distributes income annually to the trust's beneficiaries, and at the end of the trust's term or upon the death of its creator, the remaining assets are distributed to the designated charities.

These trusts have variations: the *charitable lead annuity trust* (CLAT), the *charitable remainder annuity trust* (CRAT), and the *charitable remainder unitrust* (CRUT). As you can likely tell from the names, these trusts use annuities to increase the value, income, and final distribution at the end of a specific term or upon the trust creator's death.

It's important to note that charitable trusts all have some current tax benefits and also some estate tax benefits.

An additional tax-advantaged way to reduce tax is through donation of appreciated securities. Assume for a moment that a taxpayer owns stock in a company with an unrealized gain of $25,000. By donating the stock to a qualified charity rather than selling it, paying the tax on the gain and then making a cash donation, the taxpayer has avoided paying tax on the $25,000 gain, and the taxpayer can claim a charitable deduction for the market value of the stock on the date of the gift.

5. Optimizing Capital Gains Strategies

Most taxpayers know that capital gains and losses can offset one another to arrive at a net capital gain or loss. Any capital gains are taxable. However, taxpayers can claim up to $3,000 per year in capital losses. Any excess of that amount can be carried forward indefinitely and utilized in future years until they are fully exhausted.

The tax rates for long-term capital gains—those held for more than one year—are 0% if the adjusted gross income is no more than $40,000. It jumps to 15% for adjusted gross income between $40,001 and $445,850. For adjusted gross income above that level, generally the rate is 20%. If the gains are short-term, meaning the asset was held for one year or less, they are taxed at ordinary income tax rates—the same rates as wages, interest, non-qualified dividends, and other sorts of income that vary widely.

Another capital gains tax rate to be aware of concerns the sale of collectibles. Assets such as art, jewelry, stamps and coins, antique furniture, precious metals, fine wines, and collectible cars fall into this category. Generally speaking, the capital gains tax rate on collectibles is 28%. Although 28% may seem high compared with ordinary income tax rates, this tax rate is advantageous. Compare it to the highest ordinary income tax rate of 37%. Additionally, owning assets such as collectibles that appreciate in value are often a good strategy for hedging against periods of hyperinflation.

Qualified small business stock or QSBS—the shares of a small business as defined in the Internal Revenue Code—are treated favorably for capital gains purposes, assuming both the investor and the company meet certain requirements. Those requirements include the company's incorporation in the United States as a C Corp along with gross assets of $50 million or less at all times before and immediately after the shares are issued. The company cannot be on the list of excluded business types, which include entities, hotels, restaurants, financial institutions, real estate companies, farms, mining companies, and businesses relating to law, engineering, or architecture.

Bear in mind that other requirements must be met in order to qualify. They are too numerous to list here in totality, but entrepreneurs who do qualify for tax treatment as a QSBS can benefit from enormous tax savings.

A few of my clients met the requirements, significantly reducing their capital gains taxes. They started companies that substantially increased in valuation over a period of years.

At some point the taxpayer sells all or some of the shares in a QSBS transaction.

6. Choosing the Location and Jurisdiction of Income Earning Trusts

A client of mine had established trusts for his two children in New Jersey. They were originally set up as grantor trusts so that the income earned in the trust was paid by the grantor—my client—rather than the trust. Since the trustee, who was the grantor's wife; and the beneficiaries, the grantor's children; were residents of New Jersey, this income was taxed by the state of New Jersey and by the federal government.

My client changed the trust from a grantor trust to a non-grantor trust, meaning the income from the trust would be taxed directly to the trust. He also changed the trustee from his wife to a corporation based in Delaware. Doing so placed the trust under Delaware jurisdiction. Delaware law states that if the beneficiaries don't reside in Delaware, there is no Delaware tax to be paid. New Jersey law states that even though the trust itself still resides in New Jersey, because the trustee resides outside of New Jersey, and the beneficiaries reside outside of Delaware, there is no New Jersey tax on that trust income.

The moral of the story is that even a little careful planning can lead to significant financial well-being and help you achieve generational wealth.

7. Non-Income Tax Issues for Wealthy Individuals and Families

You may have heard the term, "asset protection." What does this actually mean?

From an investment perspective, it means protecting against financial market swings. That way, when a certain threshold is reached, the financial advisor can shift the investment mix to minimize the negative impact on their clients' portfolios. Given the volatility of today's financial markets, this is a valuable form of asset protection.

From a legal and liability perspective, however, asset protection means something completely different. Many wealthy individuals can be targets of various lawsuits that could end up in judgments which deplete their assets. In order to avoid or minimize this result, many people establish asset protection trusts.

Combined with moving assets to offshore jurisdictions, an asset protection trust can effectively place assets beyond the reach of creditors and judgments. Establishing these types of trusts, as with all such vehicles, should be carefully thought out and prepared by a qualified trust and estate attorney.

8. Estate Planning

For wealthy individuals, estate planning with a qualified estate planning attorney is a must to minimize tax implications when passing assets to a spouse, the next generation, or a charity.

Currently, the combined estate and gift exemption from federal estate tax is $12.06 million per person. For a married couple, the exemption is $24.12 million. Amounts over that will potentially be subject to estate tax upon the death of the taxpayer.

Lifetime exemptions will drop to approximately $6.2 million per person at the end of 2025 due to sunset provisions in the law. Married individuals may gift any amount at any time to their spouse with no gift tax ramifications. Individuals may also gift to any other individual up to $16,000 per year without even having to file a gift tax return or using up part of the combined estate and gift tax exemption. Many parents often utilize this strategy to transfer assets to their children. A married couple may jointly gift each child $32,000 per year.

Everyone should have a will, regardless of their wealth. Otherwise, upon death, the probate courts can decide how to distribute assets. But for wealthy individuals, a will is not enough to minimize potential estate taxes upon death. A number of different kinds of trusts are often utilized to direct assets and minimize tax. Additionally, the strategy of gifting during one's lifetime can reduce the value of an estate.

It may make sense to utilize part of the lifetime gift and estate tax exemption to transfer assets to the next generation, especially if the value of those assets is or will be increasing. Once transferred, the increase, whether through income or valuation then becomes vested in the person receiving the gift.

∼

The strategies described here are often employed by wealthy individuals. It is important to note that this is by no means an exhaustive list of approaches to achieving generational wealth, but rather a source from which to provide good leadership to your team and ask the right questions of your CPA and your trust and estate attorney.

If you set up your business with these eight strategies in mind, you could be well on your way to minimizing taxes and growing your business to achieve generational wealth while cultivating the future potential of those whom you encounter along the way.

CHAPTER 9

EATING TAMALES
Love Languages in Business

Joel Clelland

Educator, Author, Speaker, and Crypto Enthusiast

When I was about 20 years old, I had tamales for the first time. My college roommate, Vince Guerrero, a trusted advisor and friend to this day, took me to a little place off the 5 Freeway in the City of Commerce, California. Rusty siding, but with clean countertops. A cozy 1950s era building off a pothole-ridden road. A smoggy day around dusk. L.A. County. It looked and smelled authentic.

Recently, Vince shared a story about *his* experience with tamales.[15]

"I remember growing up and my family making and selling tamales. A lot of tamales. Everyone would exclaim how great my parents' tamales were. It became very normal in my life to hear that, and the tamales became so familiar that they seemed ordinary. The tamales they made were just what tamales were, the picture that came to mind when someone mentioned them, as identifiable as the mental images you see when you hear the word dog or tree."

---

15   Story is based on Vince Guerrero's comments from an email to the author, June 8, 2022. Edited for length and clarity.

As a high school student, Vince received frequent invitations to friends' houses for tamales. Just as frequently, he was in for a surprise. "They would exclaim with such exuberance how good they were and how their family had made them forever. Often, I would take a bite and regret that bite, but out of respect for the relationship, I'd eat one tamale and then pretend to be completely full."

Now, with his family's help, Vince makes tamales as a side hustle—Guerrero Tamales—and sells them during the holidays. He receives plenty of orders and lots of compliments about them, but some people don't come back. He's discovered that every family and every culture has a certain approach to making tamales.

"To embrace every kind of tamale is really to embrace the things that unite us, to embrace those things that make our lives similar," he observes. "If you want to make tamales more palatable to everyone, put some cheese and sauce on them."

Through his story, Vince shares a powerful human insight that can be repurposed beyond the tamale-making business. As business leaders and entrepreneurs, we should always be looking for the "cheese and sauce" as often as it is possible to do so, looking for ways to connect with our team members, their families, and even the community at large. When we do that—when we eat the tamales and make them taste good for everyone—something powerful happens.

Eating tamales isn't really about the food, of course. It's about how we spend our most valuable asset.

Time.

Making Tamale Time

So how do we spend our time as entrepreneurs? Are we perpetually absent from the office? Are we physically present but lost in research or locked in the C-Suite? How often do we have conversations with our team members? Do we engage them in our vision and invite feedback on their progress and insights and what they are doing to help us realize our mission?

Do we ask team members how they're doing?

We give time to the things that matter most to us. If we're in and out of the office just doing the job, is it enough? Each moment we spend with our families, teammates, and customers reinforces the bond between us. Consistent, active engagement increases trust. As often as possible, take advantage of opportunities to connect with your people. If your people don't connect with you, you'll have challenges developing trust, loyalty, and mobilizing them to act.

If we let standard operating procedures and compliance get in the way of relationship-building, we'll miss the power of the human connection. You have the influence to impact your organization and community positively no matter what sector you're in, even if the language of connection isn't in the company docs.

We learn a lot and connect best when we listen and keep the lines of communication open. Strong leadership is conversational. It isn't always easy, but it's essential to make inroads with our teams, our cultures, and our community.

Lessons From Failure

Many of our greatest failures teach us the most. When I was in my twenties and still at university as an undergrad, I was like a sponge, taking in as much information as possible and making connections. As an education major, I was looking forward to becoming a teacher and getting out in the world to educate others.

I arrived at my first teaching assignment believing that I was there to share information by teaching students the course content while maintaining a level of professional distance from my stakeholders—those students and their families. That's it. I had no idea how important community connection—or "eating the tamales"—was for success.

On more than one occasion, I was asked to stop by a party, a community event, or a church gathering. Each time, I politely declined invitations to activities that were not school events, believing that by doing so, I was maintaining a professional distance. At the time, I failed to understand that when my stakeholders invited me into their lives and neighborhoods, they were really asking to connect with me and inviting me to become a part of their community.

After failing to "eat the tamales" for about six months or so, I was asked to resign due to my lack of connection. I reflected on how I had missed the powerful dynamic of connection by turning down countless opportunities to become a part of the community. Those connections could have provided foundational support for me and made me a better teacher.

Without them, I was virtually alone.

"Eating the tamales" is the act of people getting to know each other better, moving from stranger to friend or from business rep to loyal customer. Skills and certifications may get us in the room, but we need to build rapport and develop solid relationships if we want to be successful. If I had aligned with the community surrounding my school from day one, the probability of success would have been very high.

When I accepted my next opportunity in another city, I pivoted 180 degrees. That's when I recognized the "eating the tamales" concept. At times, I was literally eating tamales. At other times, I was attending birthday parties, community events, housewarming parties, neighborhood get-togethers, funerals, or other off-site gatherings.

"Eating the tamales" often includes community activities beyond a professional setting. Imagine yourself in a sports stadium and the crowd begins singing in unison, "Take me out to the ballgame." It doesn't matter what race, gender, religious, or political persuasion people are. It doesn't even matter if they're rooting for one team or the other, or who sings better. The crowd is singing one song with one voice.

They're eating one big tamale.

Let Them Feel Heard

A critical part of "eating the tamales" is listening and allowing people to tell their stories. Often, people who feel they are heard become loyal for life. Sometimes this is as simple as shutting up and not trying to fill conversational pauses with your opinions and thoughts. Silence is wisdom. If you're seeing a lot of turnover, migration, or replacement in your business, consider taking inventory of your communication approach. Where is it breaking down? Where is it seemingly nonexistent?

In business and in life, people just want to be heard.

Developing valuable soft skills like real listening, empathy, and creativity is critical. When we regularly deploy them, we let people know that we see them, and they feel appreciated.

Aside from non-negotiables such as effort, results, and a high-quality, competitive offer, the ability to connect with people is the greatest differentiator between businesses. How businesses connect with customers or clients and their businesses is the real key to long-term success and brand loyalty. Even poor communicators will be more successful than polished speakers if the people they are addressing feel cared for and heard. Listening helps stakeholders feel safe enough to lean into the difficult work—including tough conversations—and to align with what's best, even if what's best isn't the most comfortable option.

The tools and approaches we use for one person and another can differ greatly. Different people have different temperaments, and they hear and feel things in their own way. Have you ever worked with someone who used the same approach to conversation with everyone and had issues? They lost sales and pushed people's buttons, burning up relationships with business partners, family members, and friends.

People who behave this way are forgetting all about the cheese and sauce. Their integrated beliefs or practices are too rigid. "My way or the highway" doesn't build long-term rapport or buy-in. If you ever find yourself in a situation where rapport is off or seemingly non-existent, dig deeper. "I see what you mean." "Can you explain that to me?" "What else can you tell me?" "I'd like to understand what you mean but I'm not sure I get it." And, of course, "Thank you."

We can disarm people and diffuse uncomfortable situations sim-ply by asking questions or pleading ignorance, whether we're ignorant or not. Each of us can learn something new every day and in every relationship. Conditions, dynamics, people, and situations change. We must be flexible and become engaged listeners.

Ask the person in front of you if you can take notes or record the meeting.

Ask for clarification. "I'm not sure I understand what you mean," or "Can you please clarify X, Y, or Z? Thanks," will do.

Remember that tone is important too. Breathe easy. Try not to huff and puff. Smile. Ask questions and use affirming language. Be vul-nerable when necessary but never add fake humility or vulnerability. People see right through that most of the time and if that happens, your approach backfires. Rapport dissolves. Genuineness is always the best policy.

Make eye contact. Wherever we look, we are placing value. If we look away or down, we seem distracted or lacking confidence, hinder-ing our connection with others. Of course, life is filled with nuance and some cultures dissuade direct eye contact. If you plan to visit another culture, do some research into customs and expectations ahead of time.

And feel free to say, "You've got my full attention. Thank you for your patience." This is super helpful and builds rapport quickly—espe-cially if the exchange is between two very busy individuals.

Putting the Tamale Concept to Work

After my teaching experience began to make me realize that I needed to evolve, many things became easier. The ability to make connections in general was one of them. In addition to doing some basic connecting outside the workplace, I became more involved in nonprofit service, and I started an insurance practice.

Like many entrepreneurs and professionals, when I first got started in my own business, I was strongly motivated by money. A veteran agent shared something with me that proved valuable and timeless: "Through your service, they get to know you."

In the months and years that followed, I began to realize he was right. Business isn't just about making money, but about helping people, providing value, and building trust. Eventually, as I did this, my clients wanted me to be a one-stop shop, serving as everything from their financial services professional to their lawyer, plumber, and priest. It's truly amazing what happens when we develop loyalty and trust through simply doing a good job and saying yes to the tamales.

When you take time to provide people with a service they need or to educate them about a product, strategy, or something else important to them, they get to know you. They grow comfortable with you. They'll be more willing to do business with you and refer you to others. These stakeholders can be your best advocates. There are few things more powerful than a satisfied customer's testimonial.

Inside and outside of the workplace, people and dynamics can vary greatly. When I served in the cryptocurrency industry as Centric's Chief Executive Officer, I was responsible to my immediate team and our community of investors. Some of those investors wanted to break bread. Others were only interested in the money piece, the reason for their relationship with me. What had I done for them and their investment lately? What projects was I working on?

Balance in business is important. Not everyone has the same desires or wishes for the same types of connections. For the most part, people want to be effective and empowered as a team member or "in the loop" and satisfied as customers.

At the end of the day, knowing your people and their people is critical. Be sensitive to who they are and how they prefer to interact with you and your business. Things can get easier when we approach our people with their preferences in mind.

Eating the tamales isn't just about being humble or making connections. It's about making a difference by caring about who your people are.

Tamales in a Time of Crisis

The governments of the world and the media had been telling us for weeks that something bad was coming. We grasped some of the story, but not all of it.

Around lunchtime on Friday, March 13, 2020, the axe came down. Chris Suchanek, the Executive Director of Project Boon, a Southern California nonprofit focused on solving food insecurity where I served as Board Chair and continue to serve as a volunteer, called to inform me that all activities scheduled for the foreseeable future had to be canceled. In fact, the very next week, our first charity highlight event with a local NBA G-League team had to be postponed until further notice. The NBA had decided to go dark. Everything was shutting down due to a worldwide pandemic.

When a once-in-a-100 years global pandemic hits, everyone is asking, "What's next?" "How can we plan?" "What about me and my family?"

For a few days, the members of our nonprofit walked around in a daze, wallowing in mild self-pity. Most organizations like ours were sheltering in place, shutting their doors, and generally receding into zero mode—zero service, zero contact, zero impact. In that moment, we decided as an organization to ask what we can do rather than what we can't do.

Businesses, both for profit and nonprofit, were closing up shop from an abundance of extreme caution. Those of us who were having conversations about sheltering in place or proposing alternatives were being singled out as reckless.

When a fellow community leader from another nonprofit and I decided to take to the streets with toys, sweets, and essentials like toiletries, many people asked me if I was being careful. I knew what they meant by their tone. We decided that showing care and love to a community in fear was worth exposing ourselves to the virus.

My friend, an African American entrepreneur, and me, a white guy, took to the streets in search of a meaningful connection with our community. We were doing our best to "eat the tamales" in an unprecedented situation. We visited the projects and some pretty tough neighborhoods. One street we walked down had been the site of a murder the night before.

Many of the residents were happy to see us. One visit we made was to a senior living facility. An 86-year-old woman on one of the upper floors told me, "The 'rona don't come to the hood. You get in here and dance with me!"

I promptly did.

While many chose to stay indoors to avoid the virus, we asked, "How can we serve?" Whether delivering care packages to seniors, or toys, sweets, and essential items to underserved families, we made an impact. It felt good and right to act. We refused to do nothing while being as careful as possible.

During the early weeks following the closures, Project Boon leadership asked the county department of health what we could do. They suggested partnering with a restaurant with a drive-thru and passing groceries through the drive-thru window. An opportunity. A ray of hope.

A tamale.

Over the next three months, we hosted three successful events to wage our war on food insecurity, which grew more concerning week over week because of widespread closures. This did not deter Project Boon from continuing to meet the challenge. As a part-time nonprofit run by volunteers, we partnered with a restaurant and later, grocery stores. Together, we were able to push 20,000 meals out into the community in 2020.1

"Eating the tamales" means always being ready to ask, "What can we do?" "How can we serve?" "What do you need?" regardless of your central product or service. In many cases, people just want to connect, and the effort to do so breeds loyalty.

We must be ready to receive that connection in reverse as well; those who are being served also want to serve.

Our first successful drive-thru event was on Easter Sunday 2020. It renewed my belief that people have a deep desire to be seen, loved, and appreciated. We had cars lined up for one or two miles. All Project Boon workers and volunteers alike were masked-up and wearing gloves. Every car got two weeks' worth of groceries, a case or two of water, and toilet paper—as long as that lasted—and we had approximately 900 Easter baskets for the kids.

The following month, on Mother's Day, we repeated our successful campaign. Over 300 cars lined up. Groceries were distributed along with red roses for each mother. Throughout the event, our team marched up and down the line of cars passing out roses to moms while they waited with their families for the groceries.

At one point, a minor altercation broke out in the long lineup of cars. A large, honking sedan forced its way between two smaller cars. Its driver began shouting angrily. A woman stepped out of one of the smaller cars, trembling. She approached me where I stood in the middle of the street directing traffic.

"Would you like the groceries you've been waiting for?" I asked. As a board member and the head volunteer, I intended to escort her to the front of the line for her basket, and then send her on her way.

She shook her head, obviously shaken. "I'm just going to go, but I wanted to tell you that no one has ever given me, a middle-aged mom, a rose on Mother's Day."

Of all the encounters I experienced that day, this humble woman's words left the biggest impression on me. In a time filled with so much uncertainty, a simple act of kindness—sharing a rose—made an impact for good. In this woman, I saw a sister, a mom, a friend. A person who wanted to make a connection, a healthy, loving, caring, compassionate, community connection.

The Cheese and the Sauce

When people feel loved, they tend to be energized and at their best. Whether business associates, team members, or strategic members in the community, love inspires good things. Love yourself first, so you have the energy to serve. Next, love everyone else in your care by appreciating and respecting them. It's rarely all about the performance; it's about the conversations before, during, and afterward.

As leaders, we have a lot of power. How do we empower our team and community without losing control of the ship?

Model to your people what caring and connecting looks like. Figuratively speaking, "touchy feely" isn't as common as it should be in professional settings, but as leaders we can change that if we're others-focused. Expect the best from your people. Let them know that, in addition to their skill sets and ability to execute, the ability to connect with others is essential.

Sometimes the terms "empathy" and "caring" are interchangeable. Several experts in the science of soft skills refer to empathy as a key element in business leadership success.

In an article on LinkedIn's weekly newsletter, "The Future of Leadership," Marcel Schwantes calls empathy a "human superpower."[16] Empathy is a learned skill available to anyone. It's often misunderstood because there are variations of it ranging from feeling what others feel and imagining yourself in others' shoes, and imagining the world, or a situation, from someone else's point of view. "Empathy," Schwantes says, "is the cornerstone of effective servant leadership. It's about helping others feel heard and understood."

According to the findings in the 2016 DDI Report highlighted in Schwantes' article, empathy's true potential should not be

---

16   Marcel Schwantes, "The Soft Skill That Science Found Will Drive Your Leadership Performance," LinkedIn: The Future of Leadership, August 9, 2021) https://www.linkedin.com/pulse/soft-skill-science-found-drive-your-leadership-marcel-schwantes/.

underestimated. "Begin developing leaders to learn this relational skill for competitive advantage. Your ability to empathize, as a leader, will make a difference in the performance of others. And it is critical to good teamwork."[17]

As you continue eating tamales, nurture the bond of loyalty with your team, customers, and community through listening. Doing so will help you build a thriving business or practice, or take your existing endeavors to the next level.

Saying, "I care," usually isn't enough. People need to feel that you care, and they'll notice if you're pretending. We all carry emotional baggage. As a business and community leader, remember to extend empathy toward yourself, too. Eat the tamales and share them.

---

17   Evan Sinar, Ph.D., Rich Wellins, Ph.D./Richard S. Wellins, Ph.D. et al, "High Resolution Leadership: A Synthesis of 15,000 Assessments into How Leaders Shape the Business Landscape," 2016 DDI Report (DDI Development Dimensions International, Inc.) pgs. 18-23. https://media.ddiworld.com/research/high-resolution-leadership-2015-2016_tr_ddi.pdf.

CHAPTER 10

HOW TO MAKE A GLOBAL IMPACT

Dan Vega

Entrepreneur, Speaker, Business Coach, Talk-Show Host, and Investor

For business leaders who wish to make a positive global impact, there are as many different ways to amass the wealth required to move mountains and transform the future as there are people on the planet. Each individual has a unique combination of education, experience, and ideals that influence how they pursue success.

Some theories about how to generate wealth are so heavily impacted by personal perspectives or what might be considered "ideal conditions" that it becomes nearly impossible to replicate them. If an approach cannot be replicated and adapted across platforms or even across economic hurdles, then we may reach the door to generational wealth, but lack the key to unlock it.

In order to create success, our first objective must be to uphold our core values. Amassing wealth is secondary. We also know that making a true impact on the world takes resources, the likes of which won't be handed to us on a silver platter. In order to facilitate an impactful degree of wealth, it is necessary for us to have a broad client or follower base and to monetize correctly so that we can afford to grow our reach.

In his book, *Nicomachean Ethics*, the Ancient Greek philosopher, Aristotle, presented a three-step idea for principled business growth.

"*First*, have a definite, clear, practical ideal; a goal, an objective. *Second*, have the necessary means to achieve your ends; wisdom, money, materials, and methods. *Third*, adjust all your means to that end."[18]

If your goal is to solve a problem that millions of people are struggling with or to bring joy to people's lives through your talents or gifts to make a global impact, you've already met Aristotle's first requirement. Now, you must meet the other two requirements by strictly adhering to the following four steps, and the fifth step, impact, will naturally result.

Education is Key

Everything starts with acquiring an education that helps us achieve the skills and experience we need to reach our goals. Many of us have attended a university, medical school, law school, or professional programs. Still others have paid our dues and spent years self-educating, finding mentors, taking additional courses, and otherwise investing in ourselves. Whatever paths we take, the day we stop learning is the day we ensure failure.

As we educate ourselves, it is vitally important that we not only learn more skill sets that can be used as tools for our arsenal or to develop more points of leverage, but to also polish our vision of exactly what we want to accomplish as entrepreneurs and human beings. Education helps us identify systems that we can utilize to hit our goals. Education also enables us to figure out how to piece together winning strategies.

Once we have outlined a map to reach our goals, we must then

---

18   This is not a direct quote from Aristotle's work, but an often-used summary of one of its ideas. Aristotle wrote *Nicomachean Ethics* around 350 BCE, and many editions have been published since then. Philosopher Sir William David Ross (1877-1971), also known as W. D. Ross, is credited with translating the work.

reverse-engineer all that information and education and break it down to a micro-level. This enables us to create specific, actionable steps that will result in equivalent reactions until they culminate in overwhelming success.

Leverage Tools and Positioning

Upon receiving a good education, the next step is to create the right leverage tools and positioning in the marketplace. These mechanisms allow us to distribute our solution, our value, our products and services, to mass numbers of people. This may be accomplished through television, radio, writing a book, or even generating a series of articles or other content containing powerful information.

The process of creating leverage tools is not organic. It takes conscious effort to determine what tools will work best for certain goals and how we can provide value through those tools. At this stage in the process, providing value to as many people as possible is more important than trying to monetize our endeavors.

It's important to note that having a large friend base isn't necessarily a leverage tool. Some people have acquired fame with millions of followers, but when they create content, they get little to no reaction or support. Based on the number of people following their activities, that's not an engaged audience. We need a responsive audience. This is where the third step comes in.

Gaining Influence

If we're consistent, within three to six months of utilizing leverage tools, we will start to gain influence in our market or field. Without influence, even the best products and services won't make it past the planning stage to production.

If we have a large following but little response to our content, we do not have an engaged audience. But if we've chosen the right leverage tools for our target audience and we have used them consistently, we will secure a position of influence in our field. In effect, this means people have assigned us authority over a topic or a particular field in their lives.

For example, let's say Laura keeps getting marketing emails from someone we'll call Joe, who is trying to build leverage. Laura wonders, "Who is this 'Joe?'" His letters may be irritating at first, but after a while, Laura chooses to briefly review the email before deleting it. Eventually, something in one of Joe's emails catches her interest. She thinks, "Well, Joe makes a good point," or "Hey! It doesn't cost anything to accept the gift Joe is offering me, and I can glean value from it."

Once that shift happens, the recipient, Laura, assigns Joe, the email sender, a position of authority. This establishes trust between them, giving Joe some degree of influence.

Monetization Toward the Masses

The key to monetization is fully establishing the previous three steps of education, resources, and impact *before* we put any metrics or mechanisms in place to make "big money." This is where the majority of businesspeople stumble or fall. As stated, followers are not the same as an engaged audience and they give us little to no influence. If our offerings aren't monetized correctly, we won't have the necessary resources to make the impact we intend.

Making an Impact

If we successfully apply the previous four steps in the correct order—education, leverage tools, influence, and monetization—we will have all the resources we need to make a large impact on the world.

What greater calling can we have than to improve the lives of others simply by following these steps for success?

Moving Beyond Obscurity and Resistance

Performing the five steps in order and without variation is vital to success in both building generational wealth and making a significant impact on others. The reason is simple: all business owners face the same challenge when they start out. *Obscurity.* No one knows who we are or why they should pay attention to what we have to say.

Yet even after pushing through obscurity, we still must go through a phase of *resistance.* Resistance has many faces, from people who hate what we are doing and strangers telling us that we're insane, to family members who speak out against us, or potential customers who resist our products and services—even when we consistently share good products, services, or content.

The majority of people become discouraged and give up during the resistance phase. They quit, or worse, skip around the steps and only do what they feel most comfortable with. But if we face obscurity or resistance, it makes no sense to spend a lot of time and resources continuing to develop additional offerings. All that does is create a lot of valuable products that no one will ever find or buy. No trust has been established, and therefore, no influence has been gained.

Instead of investing a lot of capital in a broader range of products or services, we need to invest in tools that will help us gain a stronger leverage position and give us influence over more people at a faster rate.

The person who tries to make an impact before creating the resources to do so will become a beggar. They will constantly identify amazing causes and ways to make an impact, then have to ask others to fund these causes. Resistance is necessary. It gives us the drive we need to push through discomfort until we reach a level of *acceptance.* We most certainly can amass wealth when we have acceptance. Some of us may even hit a level of *admiration,* catapulting our impact beyond even our wildest dreams.

If we are not making the amount of money that we feel we deserve or having a broad impact, it is because we do not have a great enough influence over a sufficient number of people. This cannot be achieved simply by increasing the number of people we know. Remember, it is not how many people we know, but who know us.

The history of a highly motivating and charismatic speaker whom I'll call Robert demonstrates these points to perfection. As a former member of the military, Robert gave talks that were well-known locally for their power and ability to impact others' lives. He was as good a speaker as any around but had not made it to a national or international platform until he found a large company to hire him. He fought through the resistance phase with that company, going so far as speaking for free just to show what he could do in order to find acceptance.

Eventually, he succeeded. He gained both influence and acceptance, ultimately signing a national contract with the company to speak at different outlets across the country on a regular basis. He would travel about three days a week, speak for just a few hours, and then get to spend the rest of his time at home with his kids while waiting for his payout to arrive. By doing four speaking commitments over the course of 12 days, Robert made as much money in a month's time as some professionals made annually. That also gave him an additional two weeks per month to pursue other endeavors.

Eventually, he felt the need to do more, but family obligations kept him at home. There was no way to commit to two events per week, which would have meant traveling six out of seven days. His solution was to add value-based events for the general public while traveling for his existing contract with the company. But even though his content and delivery were outstanding, his events only drew in a handful of people.

The problem was simple. With the large company, Robert had already pushed through the resistance phase and reached acceptance, but to the public, he was still in obscurity. Rather than realizing he needed to re-evaluate the steps and gain acceptance from the general public, he decided to create other products. He spent much of his money and countless hours developing them. Although his time and money investment were certainly commendable, no one ever found his products because he had tried to monetize them before gaining influence over his new audience.

In the end, Robert had to revisit the five steps, create leverage tools for his public platforms, and work his way toward acceptance by a new client demographic before he could correctly monetize and make an impact.

Most businesspeople—from investors and speakers to authors and medical professionals—believe that they can automatically translate their reputation with existing clients into additional income by creating and monetizing new products or services. However, anyone who still faces obscurity risks spending a lot of time and resources to create valuable programs that no one will ever find.

It is imperative that we start with education and then create the right leverage tools to get the word out about our value and our solutions. We must spend an appropriate amount of time drawing others to our work and reputation by simply being in front of people on a consistent basis, solely for their benefit and without asking for anything in return. We must provide value to some aspect of their lives, eventually placing our name firmly in a position of influence and trust.

In order to monetize correctly, we should only start selling other products, services, or programs when we have a position of influence over many people. It is vital to follow the first four steps in order, without deviation, so that the fifth step—making an impact—emerges naturally. Skipping steps will create an extraordinary amount of work for mostly insignificant results.

It does not matter if we sell a product or service, or what type of industry we work in, following these five steps in order is the fastest way to generational wealth, which in turn will give us the resources we need to make a global impact.

BIOGRAPHIES

Joel Clelland

With a diverse background in education and finance, Joel Clelland is keen on partnerships, investor education, and community development. Since March 2021, Joel has served as the CEO for Centric, a cryptocurrency system working to stabilize prices and provide a global borderless medium of exchange. He also sits on the board of the community nonprofit, Project Boon, based in Southern California. Project Boon assists underserved children, individuals, and families with food security and provides connections to needed services.

Bobby Dunaway

Bobby Dunaway is the entrepreneurial publisher and CEO of Indigo River Publishing. Under his leadership, the company established a sales and distribution partnership with Simon & Schuster. He led the transformation from a hybrid publisher to a modern cooperative publisher where authors are partners in the editing, production, and marketing of their books. Bobby is committed to empowering individuals to share their wisdom through the power of story. He believes that amazing things can happen when preparation meets opportunity.

Jason Duncan

"The Real Jason Duncan" is the founder of 12 companies who got his start in entrepreneurship as an unemployed schoolteacher in 2010. Educator-turned-entrepreneur, Jason now runs a mastermind called "The Exiter Club" that helps entrepreneurs break free from the daily grind of business operations through a method he calls #ExitWithoutExiting. He is the host of *The Root of All Success* podcast, which is about the journey to success as an entrepreneur. Learn more at https://www.therealjasonduncan.com/.

Mark Hayes

With over 20 years of investing experience consisting of acquisitions, property management, urban development, and financing, Mark Hayes is the founding president of Bridge South Investments, LLC, a Nashville-based firm specializing in bridge loans for real estate and angel investing in technology, AI, healthcare, and sports and recreation. Business education is a passion for Mark as he has authored blogs, taught webinars, and is authoring a book about easy entries into real estate investing.

Matthew Holland

Matthew Holland is a serial social entrepreneur whose multi-faceted career has spanned across many market sectors: public, private, governmental, the armed forces, and non-profits. His passion, charisma, energy, and drive have led him to many tall peaks and through just as many darkened valleys. He advocates for change in the collective health system by participating on various councils and committees, and through speaking engagements, panel discussions, and writing.

Michael Markiewicz

With over 35 years of experience providing financial guidance to entertainment professionals, family offices, small businesses, and C-level executives, Michael Markiewicz is the founder and owner of Markiewicz Enterprises, LLC. His New York-based financial services company specializes in CPA services, consulting services, and asset protection. Outside of his practice, Michael is a successful investor, speaker, and is very involved with many philanthropic endeavors. He lives in Chelsea (Manhattan) with his husband Mark and their beloved wire-haired dachshunds, Maggie and Lily.

Ellen Moran

Ellen Moran is a St. Louis-based leadership consultant who has been working with national and international clients for 30 years. She is passionate about helping individuals and their teams discover, deploy, and enjoy their full range of talents while creating greater value for themselves and others. She likes reading German language newspapers to maintain her skills and observe world events through a different prism. She and her husband enjoy dancing, traveling, and being an active presence in the lives of their seven grandchildren.

Dan Vega

Dan Vega started his first business at 19 and has been writing and speaking in the field of business ever since. He has achieved success in several careers including sales, marketing, management, corporate restructuring, and consulting.

Dan is one of the top experts in the country assisting companies seeking secure funding. He now holds ownership in several successful companies and is personally invested in numerous spaces in the market including film and television, technology, health, environmental, spirits, art, and fashion.

Jayshree Vakil

Jayshree Vakil is a businesswoman, an entrepreneur, an investor, a fine artist, and a leader. Her experience as a corporate executive and entrepreneur spans a broad swath of industries ranging from technology to industrial to consumer products. She is also an award-winning fine artist specializing in semi-abstract paintings. Having started several businesses, Jayshree now mentors and encourages new entrepreneurs, especially women. She has a master's degree in advertising and bachelor's degrees in economics and fine arts.

Dr. Dan Young

Dr. Dan Young has spent over a decade serving the community as an educator, financial planner, philanthropist, community advocate, and consultant. He has a deep sense of pride about his roots and the sacrifices made by his family and people of color all over the world. Dan is quick to point out that his success is not due to his actions alone. He ascribes to the theory that it's not about how smart you are, it's about how many smart people you surround yourself with.